THE NEW FILIPINO KITCHEN

STORIES AND RECIPES FROM
AROUND THE GLOBE

EDITED BY
JACQUELINE CHIO-LAURI

PHOTOGRAPHY BY
ROWENA DUMLAO-GIARDINA

FOREWORD BY
JOHN BIRDSALL

S
SURREY
BOOKS

AN AGATE IMPRINT

CHICAGO

Printed in China

All food photography and styling by Rowena Dumlao-Giardina except for the photos on pages ix (Studio Mossige) and 98 (Tom Haga).

Editor photo by Henriette Time, Studio Hjelm.

Library of Congress Cataloging-in-Publication Data

Names: Chio-Lauri, Jacqueline, editor.
Title: The new Filipino kitchen : stories and recipes from around the globe / edited by Jacqueline Chio-Lauri ; photos by Rowena Dumlao-Giardina ; foreword by John Birdsall.
Description: Chicago : Surrey Books, an imprint of Agate Publishing, [2018] | Includes index.
Identifiers: LCCN 2018007796 (print) | LCCN 2018008924 (ebook) | ISBN 9781572848207 (e-book) | ISBN 1572848200 (e-book) | ISBN 9781572842588 (hardcover) | ISBN 157284258X (hardcover) | ISBN 9781572848207 (electronic) | ISBN 1572848200 (electronic)
Subjects: LCSH: Cooking, Philippine. | Philippines--Social life and customs. | LCGFT: Cookbooks.
Classification: LCC TX724.5.P5 (ebook) | LCC TX724.5.P5 N49 2018 (print) | DDC 641.59599--dc23
LC record available at https://lccn.loc.gov/2018007796

First printing: September 2018

10 9 8 7 6 5 4 3 2 1   18 19 20 21 22

Surrey Books is an imprint of Agate Publishing. Agate books are available in bulk at discount prices. Learn more at agatepublishing.com.

For Natividad and Sylvia,
lolas or lolos,
nanays or tatays,
who showed us strength, hope,
and love through food

CONTENTS

FOREWORD

BY JOHN BIRDSALL

W E TEND TO THINK of a cuisine as a monolithic thing, hewn from rock by ancient hands and hauled by some other generation long ago into the present, for us to passively inherit. Take cassoulet, for example. In all its local variations, it is a dish most Americans reckon as fixed in French tradition, locked in a rustic past we can't really imagine. It no longer feels like a living dish, capable of being fully modern. It's an expression of cultural nostalgia, honoring a history whose arc ended before we were born. By contrast, Filipino food—the cooking born in the island archipelago—is being carried around the world by hands that are still working and adapting their inherited culinary knowledge; Filipino food is as dynamic and fluid as molten lava, morphing to both fit and transform landscapes far from the Philippines.

Like language, the art of cooking is constantly changing as its practitioners adapt to new places, new realities.

This book of recipes—each framed by a story of discovery and re-invention—is an act of a global cuisine in the making. It's proof that cooking is a living art. Like language, it's constantly changing as its practitioners adapt to new places, new realities.

My own introduction to Filipino food came in the form of a dish my future mother-in-law made me, many years ago, on a sweltering morning in Chicago. I'd flown there from San Francisco with my new boyfriend, who had only just come out to his Ilocano parents. We'd arrived late the night before—I barely had time to exchange awkward hellos with Perry's parents before they went off to bed. The next morning, as Perry slept, I made my way to the kitchen, where his mom, Prespedina, was watching *Oprah* on a little TV set. The awkwardness of the night before was still there; it was a presence even more commanding than Oprah.

Prespedina offered me breakfast. I could have cereal, she said, or—if I wanted to—I could try "our food," as she called it: a bowl of chocolate meat. She giggled a little when she said it. Perry had told me about chocolate meat, or dinuguan. I knew that it was made with pork blood and offal. And I knew, by the way Prespedina asked, that I had to try it.

It was delicious, rich, bright with vinegar—it had soul. It represented the new realities both Prespedina and I were adapting to that morning: she, to having a gay son who had brought his boyfriend home; me, to trying a new cuisine that seemed to express both yearning for a distant homeland and an adaptation to a place of trees, sweeping green lawns, and neighbors who were mostly Irish American. On that now-distant morning, a Filipino dish was more than an expression of nostalgia. It was a single brick in the building of a new world.

John Birdsall is the author of the forthcoming book *James Beard: The Man Who Ate Too Much*. He won the James Beard Award for food and culture writing in 2014 and 2016.

INTRODUCTION

"**W**HAT IS FILIPINO FOOD?" asked my Italian mother-in-law, whose culinary repertoire doesn't stray out of the bounds of traditional Italian cooking.

I cleared my throat. I needed to buy some time to collect my thoughts before I answered. How do you define a cuisine that's a hodgepodge of numerous foreign influences and is almost as varied as the 7,000-plus islands that make up the nation?

"Umm," I said, pulling my earlobe with my thumb and forefinger, trying to silence the mocking voice in my head. "It's a mix of different kinds of cuisines."

Struggling to find the words to accurately express the complexity of my homeland's culinary traditions, I started to babble about the history of the Philippines and the many influences that molded the food, from the Malay settlers and the Chinese migrants and traders, to the Spanish and American colonizers and so on. (*Yeah, she's dying to get a Philippine history lecture.*) And about how, in general, it's not as spicy-hot as the food of nearby countries such as Thailand and Malaysia (*Right, as if she's tried Thai and Malaysian food*), though some regions in the Philippines like their dishes hot. (*Huh? Is it or is it not hot?*) And how it's heavily rice based (*Oh, she'll think risotto!*)—not like risotto, but rice cooked separately and then eaten together with another dish. (*Another dish? A Filipino dish? So back to the question "What is Filipino food?" Brava, Jacqueline! You've further alienated your mother-in-law from Filipino food!*)

My mother-in-law nodded her head, as though she understood, but I knew my explanation was anything but clear to her. She was as clueless about Filipino food as she was before she posed the question. Her nod was out of sympathy, to relieve me from my agony. She never asked me about Filipino food again.

Complex and diverse, Filipino cuisine is ineffable. Trying to define it in a few sentences will always fall short in capturing its essence. To make

Trying to define Filipino cuisine in a few sentences will always fall short in capturing its essence.

sense of Filipino food, it has to be experienced, with all the emotions and sensations that are associated with it.

If only I had thought to tell my mother-in-law my story about torta, or omelet, a favorite childhood dish. If only I told her about my lola (grandma) pounding the heads she severed from fresh shrimp in the kitchen while her transistor radio blared melodrama. How the rich, tomalley-like flavor she extracted from the shrimp heads perked up the dish's flavor. How she cleverly packed the stovetop frittata with as much substance as flavor to balance our diet and feed three families on a shoestring budget. The way she relentlessly beat egg whites with a fork from goo to stiff foam with the same hand she used to beat us, her grandchildren, to form us into better shapes of ourselves. The way she made an insignificant, unremarkable egg strong enough to hold a cornucopia of ingredients together. And why—after many years have passed, and mindsets on child-rearing and good eating have changed—my memories of torta embody love without fear, flavor without bitterness.

A story, in addition to preparing the dish for my mother-in-law to see, smell, taste, and feel, would have given her a far better understanding of and connection to Filipino food than any definition I could have strung together. I missed out on what could have been a great opportunity to break the cultural barrier that stood between me and the other woman in my husband's life.

An understanding, a connection, and—most of all—an experience. These are what the stories and recipes in this book will put on the table. As food is inevitably entwined with life, this book is as much about people as it is about food.

Certain dishes evoke memories that, when explored, lead to heartwarming revelations. For me, the sound of a stone pestle crashing into a mortar; the smell of garlic, onions, and fresh shrimp extract simmering in a wok; the golden color and halo shape of a torta; the springy texture of the cooked beaten egg; the steam, caramelized minced meat, and brightly colored bits of vegetables that escape when the torta is sliced; and the savory yet subtly sweet first bite steer me back to the pains and joys of my childhood. When I examine different parts of my life through the lens of torta, I discover empathy and reconciliation.

I asked the book's contributors to share memories and epiphanies accessed through Filipino food. To take their reflections further, each of them developed a recipe inspired by a Filipino dish that means a lot to them. Even though the dishes are common in the Philippines,

As food is inevitably entwined with life, this book is as much about people as it is about food.

every contributor put his or her own stamp on it. While most may have evolved in varying degrees from the traditional Filipino versions to suit the author's new way of life, all are, nevertheless, anchored to an authentic Filipino experience.

I am awed by the contributions of these men and women. They spoke from the heart and cooked from the soul. As I read and edited their stories, I felt their emotions, saw their worlds through their eyes, and walked in their shoes. As I tested and tasted the recipes, I was drawn to a deeper appreciation of the cuisine's versatility and the people's resilience. Our food has been shaped by indigenous hands that, when exposed to hundreds of years of foreign influences, adopted and adapted what they could to their means and liking. The result was a cuisine— morphed in the homeland, distinct from its origins. As millions of Filipinos have traveled abroad and set down roots beyond the archipelago of 7,641 islands, our food, as exemplified by the recipes in this book, persists—and, in fact, is gaining the recognition it deserves in the mainstream. I don't think it's because the dishes resist change. It's because they and the people who create them are able to adapt to new environments and new times, while staying true to themselves. Borrowing the words of Franklin D. Roosevelt: "There are many ways of going forward, but only one way of standing still."

This collection is a buffet. Emotions and flavors from bold to subtle, rustic to refined, and everything in between blaze, just like the cuisine. But though each piece recounts a unique, deeply personal experience, all speak of truths that are universal.

I hope that this book will help you understand what Filipino food is about in a more profound way—the way you would experience it if a Filipino family member or friend told you about it. If you, like my mother-in-law, are not familiar with the cuisine, this book will shed light; if you are familiar with the food, you will see dishes in a light you've never seen them in before. But, most of all, I hope that through this book, you will join us in embracing our differences and celebrating our commonalities—regardless of your food beginnings.

ABOUT THE RECIPES

The recipes in this book are developed with you in mind—an openminded person who, every now and then, is in search of heightened food experiences. They are for those who'd like to have a taste of Filipino food at home—wherever that may be—without having to travel far to shop for ingredients, without having to cook for hours on end in the kitchen, and without having to possess special culinary expertise.

Most of the ingredients in this book are available in grocery stores or in the Asian food aisle of major supermarkets. A few of the ingredients in some of the recipes, however, may be found only in Asian grocery shops. Though Asian shops dot every part of the world, we give you an option to use easier-to-find alternatives for these ingredients, in case a trip to one might not be convenient.

Even if they're available in shops, it's difficult to find ingredients if you don't know what you're looking for. In the box below, you'll find an introduction to some of the less-familiar items used in the recipes in this book, all of which are available only in Asian grocers unless specified otherwise.

Remember, pleasure can be derived not only in eating, but in preparing food as well. I suggest you read the personal narrative before following each recipe. This way you can relive the contributor's story as you recreate the dish, which will enhance your Filipino food experience. Who knows where this exploration of the senses may lead? Perhaps to a whole new memorable story and recipe of your own.

Mabuhay!

ANNATTO SEEDS (ATSUETE OR ACHUETE): rust-red seeds of the annatto used as natural food coloring; smaller than unpopped popcorn kernels. Also available in Latin markets and in the international aisle of some supermarkets.

BAGOONG ALAMANG: fermented shrimp paste, sold in jars. Bagoong, in general, is fermented seafood paste. There are different varieties depending on the kind of seafood used, but bagoong alamang is the most common.

BAGOONG MONAMON: fermented salted anchovy sauce, sold in jars.

BANANA BLOSSOM: purplish tear-shaped banana heart, about the size of a football.

BANANA KETCHUP: made from mashed bananas but looks like tomato ketchup because of the food coloring used; sold in bottles like ketchup.

BANANA LEAVES: sold folded in bags in the refrigerated or frozen section of Asian grocers; enhance the flavor of food wrapped and cooked in them and serve as natural foil or parchment paper.

BIHON (BIJON) NOODLES: thin, dry rice noodles also known as rice vermicelli; in general, they do not need to be soaked; cook according to package directions.

BITTER MELON (AMPALAYA): rough, greenish-skinned, elongated gourd.

CALAMANSI: Philippine lime, similar in color but smaller than a regular lime. Turns yellow-orange as it matures.

CHAYOTE: greenish-yellow, pear-shaped squash.

CHICHARRON: pork rind or crackling. Also available in supermarkets.

CHORIZO DE BILBAO: a dense, semi-dry, spicy sausage.

FISH SAUCE (PATIS): amber-colored liquid sold in bottles; a few drops lift a dish's umami flavor. Also available in supermarkets.

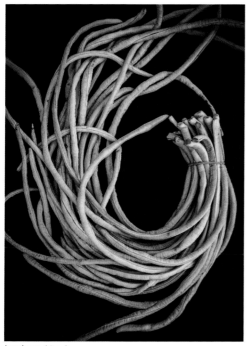

long beans (sitaw)

okra

GLUTINOUS RICE FLOUR: also called sweet or sticky rice flour; has a higher starch content than regular rice flour, which makes it better for thickening sauces.

GRATED CASSAVA (KAMOTENG KAHOY): also called yuca; sold in frozen packs.

GREEN MANGO: unripe mango.

GREEN PAPAYA: unripe papaya.

JACKFRUIT (LANGKA): ripe, sweet, bright yellow fruit sold in cans in syrup; not to be confused with the canned green, young jackfruit packed in brine or water.

LONG BEANS (SITAW): yard-long beans.

LONG (ASIAN) EGGPLANT: long and slim, in contrast to the round, voluptuous Italian eggplant.

MORINGA (MALUNGGAY): leaves of the horseradish tree.

OKRA: also called lady's finger, a long, five-sided green pod with a pointed end. Also available in the fresh produce section of some supermarkets.

PIGEON PEAS (KADYOS OR KADIOS): tropical peas; sold frozen in bags. Also available in Indian food shops as toovar lilva.

SPLIT MUNG BEANS (SPLIT BALATONG OR MONGGO): small, yellow legumes (whole, unsplit monggo beans are dark green); sold dry.

SWEET RICE: also called glutinous or sticky rice. It is gluten-free, despite the name. Its starchiness gives it a more opaque white color than regular rice and makes it suitable for preparing Filipino sweets and rice cakes.

SWEET RICE POWDER: coarser than glutinous rice flour; can be made by grinding uncooked sweet rice in a blender or coffee grinder.

UBE HALAYA: jam made from boiled, mashed purple yams; sold in jars.

WATER SPINACH (KANGKONG): also called swamp cabbage or, in some Asian shops, morning glory or ong choy; the green stems and either narrow elongated or arrow-shaped leaves of a semi-aquatic plant.

WINGED BEAN (SIGARILYAS): four-cornered bean sold fresh; has a milder flavor than a snow pea or green bean.

banana blossom

bitter melon (ampalaya) >

chayote

winged bean (sigarilyas)

split mung beans (split balatong or monggo)

calamansi

< annatto seeds (also atsuete or achuete)

moringa (malunggay)

A WORD ON FILIPINO CUISINE AND CULTURE

This book is not a traditional cookbook or guidebook to Filipino cuisine. It is designed so that you may discover the nuances of Filipino cooking organically, through the stories and recipes of people who champion it—wherever they may live. However, there are a few concepts that are important in Filipino food culture; in many ways, they illustrate that it has always been fundamentally adaptable and inclusive yet also individualized.

Some people like to talk about Filipino food as a "fusion" of Eastern and Western customs and ingredients. Like many other cultures, it is often at the center of our celebrations, and everyday meals tend to be sit-down family affairs. But unlike Western tradition, Filipino meals are typically served family style, not course by course.

There tends to be a strong sense of inclusivity when it comes to meals: everyone is welcome. Meals traditionally consist of kanin (cooked rice) and one or more ulam (main dishes) that are served from communal platters set in the middle of the table. Though kanin and ulam are cooked separately, they usually taste better when eaten together and shared with loved ones.

One trademark of Filipino food culture is the sawsawan (dipping sauces), a variety of which are typically served on the side. These condiments cover a range of tastes—spicy, salty, savory, sour, sweet, umami, or a combination of some or all—and allow diners to adjust the flavor profile of the food to their individual liking. So don't worry: concoct and take any sawsawan as you please. It won't be taken as an insult to the cook. The goal is to embrace each diner's individuality and to satisfy all who partake in the meal.

Before the Spanish and American conquests, native Filipinos ate meals kamayan, or with their hands. Most Filipinos use cutlery these days, but it's not uncommon for some to still eat this way in their homes. Likewise, one can now find Filipino restaurants and pop-up events that recreate the kamayan experience by serving vast spreads of food on banana leaf–lined communal tables from which diners dig in with their hands.

CHAPTER 1

SEAFOOD

FISH AND RICE is the traditional meat and potatoes of a Filipino diet. A nation of 7,641 islands spread over waters that partly make up the Coral Triangle, the Philippines is endowed with a rich assortment and concentration of marine life. Naturally, many of the varieties of seafood used in Philippine kitchens—such as bangus (milkfish), lapu-lapu (grouper), and suaje (endeavor prawn)—are indigenous to its geographic location and may be difficult to find in other parts of the world. The dishes in this chapter, however, demonstrate the resilience of the cuisine and the people who prepare it. Without sacrificing its hallmark Filipino flavors, each recipe is adapted to use the freshest fish, shellfish, and ingredients that are likely to be found in your area. It is equally worth mentioning that the cooking techniques here are not exclusive to seafood and will work just as well with other types of protein. Even kinilaw, a raw fish preparation, can be made with meat, but with the addition of subjecting the meat to heat before curing.

TEACH A GIRL TO FISH

{AS TOLD TO THE EDITOR}

A STRONG BITE. A frenzied whirring of the reel. A whiskered aquatic creature splashed through the surface of the river and thrashed about, dangling at the end of a bent rod. It was a climactic moment for my cousins and me as we sat on the edge of the river side by side on a warm sunny day, fishing poles in hand, eyes and mouths wide open.

I was about 10, and camping by the river with my stepdad's big family was an every-weekend affair. During the day, we fished, swam, and boated through waters that sparkled like tinsel. On the boat, Grandpa assembled a crate with baited hooks, which he released onto the water to troll for catfish. He reeled in enough fish to feed a hungry mob. I watched with horrified fascination as he gutted the horned pout, cut through its skin around the head and the shoulder blade, and pulled the skin off with pliers. For the grand finale, Grandpa sprinkled salt on the fish, prompting the headless, gutless, and skinless body to leap into the air and dance a postmortem jig.

I was not born in this land of plenty. I was no stranger, however, to rivers and fish. I was born in the Philippines and was transplanted to the United States when my mother married my stepfather, who was in the Marines. Although I was only five when we moved, I would never forget the life we left behind in the third world.

"I'm begging you," Grandmother had said to my mother in Tagalog. "Leave your daughter here with me." Her voice had choked with desperation when she found out about our impending immigration to the United States.

CRISTINA QUACKENBUSH was born in Malabon in Manila, Philippines. At the age of five, she moved with her mother to Evansville, Indiana, where she was raised near her step-grandmother's farm. Her mother's cooking sustained her throughout her childhood, while her grandmother taught her a farm-to-table lifestyle. As an adult, Cristina held various positions at restaurants managing both kitchens and the front of the house with prominent New Orleans chefs. In 2012, with the encouragement of Chef Adolfo Garcia, Cristina began her journey toward opening the doors to Philippine cuisine in the Crescent City.

But how could Mom do that? Asking her to leave me—her only child—was unthinkable. It would have meant depriving me of a chance for a better life. The place my grandmother referred to as "here" was in the slums of Malabon in Metro Manila.

Malabon lies along the lowlands of Manila Bay, near the mouths of three vast rivers. Once dotted by ponds swarming with fish, the area was then crammed with shacks swarming with hungry squatters. Often, sewage water pooled on open surfaces, discharging a putrid smell. Clusters of tiny, box-type huts sprouted along muddy, narrow alleys on the tidal terrain, and the lack of proper drainage guaranteed flooding as often as rainfall on our tropical archipelago.

But sunshine filled the place each morning when I saw Grandmother. As soon as I got up from the wicker mat that was our bed, there she was. Love beamed from her every smile, every word, and every touch. She took care of me like I was her very own, spoiled me beyond her meager means, treated me like a princess.

As a family of 10—Grandma, great-uncles, cousins, Mom, and me—we crouched around the coffee table in our teetering shanty during mealtimes. Our single-room dwelling reeked of fish. We didn't have a refrigerator, just as we didn't have plumbing, a dining table and chairs, beds, or the space to house basic furniture. We had survived mostly on meals of fish and rice.

By the river in Indiana, my cousins and I skittered back to camp at dusk. Twigs crunched under our feet while the unmistakable whiff of fish grilling on charcoal wafted to our noses. Dinner that night was celestial. Cooked fish was the star of the supper for everyone except my mother. She preferred a dish called kinilaw, a vinegar-cured raw fish. Unlike the rest of us, Mom chowed down with gusto on rice and catfish kinilaw, which was marinated in vinegar, red onion, cucumber, and tomatoes.

Mom's zest for kinilaw didn't arouse my appetite for the dish. The thought of eating uncooked fish made me squirm with disgust. Like most people in the United States at that time, I had developed a phobia of ingesting anything raw. Moreover, how could I stomach raw catfish after I had witnessed it being caught and butchered? To me, eating uncooked fish was barbaric, unhygienic, and a precursor to illness.

Mom reminded me that this was a dish we used to have in the Philippines. I was too little to remember, but according to her, it was a common dish back home because preserving food in vinegar had been more affordable and feasible for us than owning a fridge. Vinegar also gave the fish flavor and texture. If salt could make a fish dance, vinegar could make a dish sing.

Vinegar gave the fish flavor and texture. If salt could make a fish dance, vinegar could make a dish sing.

After dinner, we sat around a campfire, roasting marshmallows under a dome of glittering stars. The prospect of sleeping in the wilderness excited me. I retired to the tent and lay down on the floor, just as we had done in the Philippines. Intoxicated by the day's happenings and lulled by frogs croaking, leaves rustling, and water swishing, I dozed off, cradled by Mother Nature.

My apprehensions about eating kinilaw dissipated only years later. I discovered that vinegar, an acid, is liquid fire. Like heat, it cooks the fish and kills pathogens. When it comes to adding flavor and enhancing the presentation of the dish, the possibilities are limitless. Who would have known that I would one day open the only Filipino restaurant in New Orleans, and that my version of kinilaw would be a star of the menu?

To Latin Americans, kinilaw is like ceviche. To Hawaiians, it's known as poke. To Guamanians, it's kelaguen. To me, a chef born in the Philippines and raised in the Midwest, kinilaw is about keeping an open mind and taking chances. If I had let my prejudices hold me back, God knows what I would have missed. It would probably have been as unthinkable as turning down my opportunity to relish life in the US of A.

A wise man once said, "Give a man a fish, and you feed him for a day; teach a man to fish, and you feed him for a lifetime." I say, "Teach a girl to fish, and she will feed you for a lifetime." ◆

KINILAW

VINEGAR AND CITRUS—CURED FISH WITH
COCONUT MILK AND GREEN MANGO

According to folklore, kinilaw, one of the most ancient of Filipino foods, dating back to the pre-Spanish era, was first concocted when a king asked his trusted cook to prepare a dish like no other. It was then that kinilaw—or food that has been "cooked" with acid without the use of heat—was hatched. It was a royal success! This dish is usually served as pulutan, an appetizer accompanied by a beverage.

PREPARATION TIME: 15 minutes + 1 hour to marinate

YIELD: 6–8 servings

3 pounds best-quality firm-fleshed fish fillets (such as black drum), cut into bite-size cubes

1 cup coconut vinegar or white vinegar

1 cup freshly squeezed calamansi juice or lime juice (from about 25 calamansi or 12 limes)

1 tablespoon kosher salt

1 large knob ginger, peeled and grated

4 Thai chiles, seeded and sliced vertically

1 medium red onion, cut into thin slivers

1 green mango, peeled, pitted, and cut into thin slivers

1 green bell pepper, seeded and cut into thin strips

1 red bell pepper, seeded and cut into thin strips

1 (14-ounce) can coconut milk

1 bunch cilantro leaves, for garnish

Put the diced fish in a mixing bowl and add the vinegar, calamansi juice, salt, ginger, chiles, and onion and toss well. Cover with plastic wrap and let the fish marinate in the refrigerator for up to 1 hour.

Add the mango, green and red bell peppers, and coconut milk to the fish mixture and mix well. Serve immediately, garnished with the cilantro.

GOOD FOR ONE

BESIDES MY COMPULSIVE QUEST for Mr. Right, there was something else I wouldn't be caught dead admitting in my mid-20s: I hated being around couples. This ill feeling was rooted in envy, which we Catholics condemn as a deadly sin. It could be serious enough to bar me from deliverance from the fires of hell—a cross too heavy for me to bear.

The problem was, I couldn't just ignore or avoid couples. I ran a seafood restaurant that nurtured them and provided the perfect setting for a Romeo and a Juliet to gaze into each other's eyes, set the mood to wine, dine, and whisper sweet nothings, and celebrate coupledom with a menu including clichéd aphrodisiacs and a signature dish for two.

Let's take Table 14, for instance—a twosome's favorite corner, one of the snuggle-up nooks in the restaurant. The booth was semi-enclosed by lateen sails that swayed gently with the breeze from the overhead air-conditioning vents. To top it all off, a forget-me-not-blue pendant lamp hung over the middle of the table, accentuating the adoring look in each lovebird's eyes.

It had been over a year and a few failed relationships since I had moved to Dubai. When I landed the job as restaurant manager in a renowned five-star hotel, I welcomed it. At age 24, two consecutive broken engagements had tossed me into singlehood—when most of my contemporaries, including my older and younger sisters, had families of their own. Flying solo was more appealing to me than being a third wheel, and so I headed to Dubai for the job and to escape from home, where I no longer belonged.

Voices of guests engaged in tête-à-têtes vied with Kenny G's sax softly serenading in the background. The couple's chatter at Table 14 would hush as I approached.

"This is our menu," I would announce, with a wide smile pasted on my face. I gestured toward a wood-framed, sultry blue board that was hand-printed with fiery yellow paint. It was mounted on a dhow-shaped structure on wheels that was almost as tall as my five feet two inches, and almost as heavy as my 100 pounds. I would allow my audience to ooh and aah at its uniqueness before proceeding to explain what we had to offer.

I must have recited the menu as often as the Hail Marys of a hundred rosaries: the freshly shucked oysters, the caviar, the mezzes from around the world, our own twist on bouillabaisse and other types of soup, the selection of seafood dishes prepared in Far Eastern and Mediterranean styles, and the display of the day's fresh catch from which guests could choose the fish they wanted, cooked in any way they liked. Diners looked thrilled as I recited my script, though to myself, I sounded like a broken record.

"Last but not least is the restaurant's signature dish," I would continue. "It's char-grilled lobster, salmon and hammour fillets, and deep-fried tiger prawns with your choice of beurre blanc, garlic pepper, or red chile sauce. The dish is good for two."

That platter would have been enough to feed a small family in my homeland, the Philippines. Seafood abounds in the nation of islands, but this kind of variety was unusual—lobster and salmon never appeared on our table, and we ate prawns and hammour, aka lapu-lapu,

JACQUELINE CHIO-LAURI has more than eight years' experience in the food industry. She has opened and managed restaurants at deluxe hotels, such as Shangri-La and Sheraton. While working in Dubai, she was one of the five young women professionals featured in *Emirates Woman* magazine in a special report, "Why the Future Is Female." Jacqueline's writing has been published in anthologies and compilations, such as *Chicken Soup for the Soul: Find Your Inner Strength*. Her short memoir, "Good for One," from which this story has been adapted, won the short memoir writing competition at WomensMemoirs.com and was published in the anthology *Tales of Our Lives: Fork in the Road*. She founded the website *My Food Beginnings* to fire up an appetite for Filipino food worldwide. For now, Jacqueline lives in Norway, with her one and only husband, child, and cat.

only rarely. It was the beloved national fish bangus, or milkfish, that dominated our home menu. Though bonier than sea bass, its crowning glory is its melt-in-the-mouth black belly fat and unshrinkable, tasty skin. Bangus has many homey variations, including daing, in which it is marinated with vinegar and then fried, and sometimes paksiw, in which it is stewed in vinegar. However, the bangus dish that is as emblematic to our family as the sign of the cross is to our religion is bulanglang, nationally known as sinigang sa bayabas, a subtly sour, sweet, and savory soup flavored with guavas.

When a couple ordered the seafood platter, two waiters would burst out from the kitchen, each carrying one end of a three-foot-long metal dish fitted with marble slabs. The smell of char-grilled seafood would permeate the room, and guests would purr as they watched the dish being served. "Madam, sir, the seafood platter," the waiter would announce, placing the heavy dish on the table.

After I finished taking the orders, I pushed the menu board to another table. Like some form of temporal punishment, it was a man and a woman, another pair of lovebirds. The scene looked familiar. Swept off her feet, the woman had probably left everything behind—her job, her family, and her fiancé—for this man who promised her forever. Little did she know that when the relationship would sour, the man would shut her out of his life without so much as a goodbye. *Oh joy*, I thought, *when will this torture ever end?*

Boo-freaking-hoo! chimed another unsympathetic voice. *Shame on you! As if you haven't been raised by strong single mothers. . . .* The voice had a familiar ring. The same words would have come firing out of the mouth of Lola, my grandma and our family's matriarch, had she known of my ordeal.

Lola, like my mother, was widowed in her 30s. She had been cast into a lifetime of singlehood in 1944, during World War II, when Japanese soldiers barged through the door of her home in Pampanga and dragged Lolo, her husband and my grandfather, out of the house. They tied him to a tree for all the neighbors to see what befell a person who supported the resistance. There, a Japanese soldier beat Lolo without mercy, then shoved him onto the back of a truck. Lola, mother of five young children and one on the way, ran to the truck. Before she could reach it, she fell to the ground unconscious, unable to say goodbye. The truck carrying Lolo pulled away.

Lola attempted in vain to see Lolo at the garrison where he was held prisoner, every time bringing whatever food she could scrape up for him. Once, it was a bowl of sinigang sa bayabas, Lolo's favorite. As she always did, she left the food with the prison guard, trusting it would be delivered to her husband. Weeks later, someone leveled with her. An insider told her about the sinigang she had brought; the guard, tantalized by the soup's aroma, helped himself to it. Lolo struggled with the guard for the dish, and the guard's bayonet pierced Lolo's side, leaving a wound that would lead to his death. Lolo had fought out of hunger, not just for the food he loved, but for everything the dish embodied: the love of his wife, of his family, and of freedom.

Lola never got to say goodbye, never found Lolo's remains, never remarried. Yet, she lived a full life. Who was I to whine?

I had to embrace my singlehood. But the truth was, that's easier said than done, especially when my biological clock ticked, "Time is running out." And haven't I mentioned? This was in the mid-'90s in Dubai, where it was common to see women wrapped in black chadors, even at temperatures over 104°F, and where appearing in public alone often attracted unwanted attention. Once, in my conservative one-piece swimwear, I had lain down and closed my eyes for a moment on a tranquil beach with sand as white and fine as confectioners' sugar. When I opened my eyes, faces of bearded men in dishdashas greeted me. They scrutinized me as if I were merchandise at an open-air souk. When I drove, men sometimes hurled slurs at me: "Filipina, f--- you!" And before I could buy myself a car, a taxi driver once groped my leg in his cab. Don't get me wrong, I was no beauty queen, but in Dubai, I could turn some heads even if I was buttoned up to my neck and covered down to my ankles simply because I was an unaccompanied Asian female.

Nevertheless, I worked hard on staring down my fear of feeling inadequate and the social stigma by which my world judged me. I decided to gear up and brave it out. When I wasn't at work, I ate at restaurants, jogged along the corniche, and went to the beach—on my own. Yes, I still sustained a mix of ogling, pitying, and disdainful looks, but sooner or later, life began to taste better.

Eventually, the day came when the smile on my face as I spoke with guests at the restaurant was heartfelt. And my automatic replies of "Excellent" to the common greetings of "How are you?" rang true. The torture had ended. The presence of couples didn't bother me anymore. A glow of life sparked within me.

One busy Thursday night, a man seated at Table 14 caught my attention. His eyes were lowered on the lavosh crackers and marinated olives he nibbled with his martini. I took the chance to examine his features from where I stood: dark short hair, angelic face hardened by a determined look, and a long, straight nose that gave away his origins—French or Italian, I supposed.

"Miss Jackie," one of my staff reminded me, "Table 14 hasn't seen the menu yet."

I pushed the dhow board toward Table 14.

I delivered my speech as usual, ending with the restaurant's signature seafood dish.

"Do you have anything against people who eat alone?" asked the man.

If you only knew . . . , I thought. Before I could answer, he continued, "Why is your specialty dish good for two?" His caramel-colored eyes shifted from the board to me. *I'd die to have long eyelashes like his.*

"That's not a problem," I said, "For you, we can make it good for one."

I scribbled his order on a docket and marked the seafood platter FOR ONE in all caps, underlined twice—there was a time when I had to butt heads with the chef before he agreed to prepare this dish just for one. Thank God, times and circumstances had changed.

That man would turn out to be the one. Years later, we would share seafood platters, sinigang, all types of food, and life. I consider myself truly blessed, not only for meeting my soul mate, but especially for meeting him when I did. ◆

SEAFOOD SINIGANG

SOUR AND SAVORY SEAFOOD SOUP
SEASONED WITH GREMOLATA

Sinigang is adobo's close contender for the title of National Dish of the Philippines. It has many variants, depending on the fruit that sours the dish. Commonly used are sampaloc (tamarind), ka-mias (bilimbi), bayabas (guava), and calamansi (Philippine lime)—fruits grown in Philippine soil. Unfortunately, these fruits are difficult to find in the countries where I've lived. Hence, I recreated this dish using the all-year-round, easy-to-find lemon. Like many Filipino dishes, this soup is bold in taste: sour, salty, slightly sweet, spicy, and umami. For a more flavorful stock, reserve the shells and heads of the shrimp or prawns, simmer with the stock for at least 10 minutes, then strain. For an extra zing, I season sinigang with what I call a Filipinized gremolata, a mildly modified version of the Italian condiment made with parsley, lemon zest, and fried—instead of raw—garlic. This dish, which reminds me of home and heritage, can be prepared using just one pot. The recipe is easy to scale, whether you're cooking for a village or just for one.

PREPARATION TIME: 45 minutes

YIELD: 4 servings

GREMOLATA

1 tablespoon extra virgin olive oil

4 small cloves garlic, finely chopped

1 bunch flat-leaf parsley, finely chopped

Grated zest of 2 lemons

SINIGANG

4 cups seafood stock or water with dissolved fish bouillon cubes

Juice of 1 lemon, plus more to taste

1 teaspoon granulated sugar

2 red onions, chopped

4 tomatoes, chopped

1 pound fish fillets (such as salmon, monkfish, or cod), cut into 4 pieces

½ pound long beans or green beans, trimmed and cut into 1-inch pieces

4 fresh whole chiles of your choice

1 bunch water spinach or spinach, thick stems removed

Fish sauce, to taste

1 pound mixed shellfish (such as prawns, shrimp, and crab claws), shelled and cooked

Cooked rice or crusty bread, for serving

Make the gremolata: In a 3-quart saucepan, heat the olive oil over medium heat until it shimmers. Add the garlic and cook until it is light golden, then immediately remove the pot from the heat. Transfer the garlic mixture to a bowl and let it cool for 1 minute. Mix with the parsley and lemon zest. Set it aside.

Make the sinigang: Pour the seafood stock into the same saucepan used to fry the garlic. Add the lemon juice and sugar and bring the mixture to a boil over medium heat. Add the onions and tomatoes. Cover the pan, reduce the heat to low, and simmer for 5 minutes, or until the onions are translucent and the tomatoes are mushy.

Recipe continues >

Put the fish in a strainer or colander and dunk it into the simmering broth. Cook for 3 to 5 minutes, until opaque throughout. Be careful not to over-cook it. Immediately transfer the fish to a plate and set it aside.

Put the beans in the strainer and dunk it into the simmering broth. Cook for about 5 minutes, or until the beans are tender but still vibrant green. Transfer the beans to a plate and set it aside.

Put the chiles and water spinach in the strainer and dunk it into the simmering broth. Cook for about a minute, or until they are tender but still vibrant in color. Transfer the chiles and spinach to a plate and set it aside.

While the broth continues to simmer, taste and add fish sauce and more lemon juice as needed. Distribute and arrange the fish, shellfish, and vegetables into each of four bowls.

Remove the broth from the heat and ladle it into the bowls with the seafood and vegetables. Sprinkle each serving with the gremolata. Serve the soup piping hot, with rice or crusty bread.

SMOKE GETS IN MY EYES

J EEZ, MY EYES were smoked! I called it quits, at least for the day, and turned off the computer. The first rays of sunrise had already peeked out of the dark Italian skies. My eyes were puffy with fatigue and lack of sleep. Lying in the bed next to my desk was my big fluffy Maremmano—our only child, so to speak. He could finally get the peace and quiet he deserved, free from the clickety-clacking of the keyboard. I hugged him goodnight before leaving the room and retiring to my own bed.

I'd been at it for nights. It's as if I were possessed by this *Fatal Attraction*–like obsession with tropical plants endemic to the Philippines. For hours on end, I sat in front of my monitor and scoured the Internet in search of that elusive genie—the online stockist that could grant me my horticultural wishes.

It was 2001, two years since my move to Italy. My husband and I were just getting settled in our new home in Fiumicino, close to the airport in Rome, after living at his parents' house in Lido di Ostia, an urban residential quarter that was more concrete than green. In contrast, our new residence had plentiful communal and private spaces for verdant life. Immediately, I knew what kind of plants I would like to cultivate in our garden. Unfortunately, they weren't the kind that grew naturally in Italy.

The native plant life in my new home country was very different from that of my motherland. But I believed that if I, Philippine-born and -raised, could thrive in Italy, then so could the flora I was used to. I set my mind to recreating a mini–tropical paradise on Mediterranean soil. Getting Philippine plants into the country proved to be a dead end, so I kept

ROWENA DUMLAO-GIARDINA is a food, wine, and travel blogger, recipe developer, and food photographer and stylist. Her work has appeared in the *Huffington Post*, *Bon Appétit*, *Glamour*, *Vanity Fair*, and CNN. Her personal blog is *Apron and Sneakers*. Rowena is the daughter of the late Captain Ramon Dumlao, a pilot who airdropped relief goods for the United Nations. Her father's tragic death in 1999 while on duty in Angola led her on a solo soul-searching trip to Europe—where she met her Italian husband.

my hope alive by tracking down purveyors of seeds. Sure, the path from minute seeds to lush leaves would be long and uncertain, but I was up for it, regardless of whether I turned out to have green or black thumbs.

As the saying goes, "Seek and you will find." So, seek and seek I did until one day, I was rewarded. At last I found a plant shop in the United Kingdom that could ship to Italy. If my sheepdog weren't so heavy, I would have lifted him up and swung him around the room with a resounding "Weehee!"

Online shopping for rare seeds was like going to the supermarket on an empty stomach—everything I saw turned to a must-buy! After numerous clicks of the mouse, my shopping basket filled up fast, and my total amount to pay mushroomed to an outrageous sum. In the end, common sense and cost considerations prevailed. I cut back the list to what I regarded as the most essential: *Pandanus amaryllifolius* (pandan), *Moringa oleifera* (malunggay), *Citrofortunella microcarpa* (calamansi or Philippine lime), *Psidium guajava* (guava), *Strelitzia reginae* (bird of paradise), *Mimosa pudica* (makahiya), *Ixora coccinea* (santan), and of course, not to be missed, the star of the tropics: the beautiful and beloved banana.

Sad to say, I had little luck in keeping many seedlings alive. I nursed them like fragile babies, cheered them on when they displayed wee dots of sprouting leaves, and mourned over those that ended up in the dustbin. What adapted to their new environment were the guava, moringa, bird of paradise, and—whew—the banana.

Days whizzed into years. My husband and I bore two children. Meanwhile, I watched my young, warmth-loving specimens grow into hardy trees and eventually saw them bear the fruits of my labor. Growing up in a climate with four seasons, these trees behaved differently from their counterparts in their natural habitat. The moringa, for example, usually an evergreen, became deciduous in a nontropical climate; I got to pick its leaves only in the summer. Likewise, after its beautiful flowers blossomed, the guava tree failed to move on to the fruiting stage. As for the spectacular bird of paradise, it flowered only in the summer, while the banana, regal in structure with its large, fanlike foliage, never yielded a heart. But that was fine with me, since the banana tree provided the key ingredient to prepare a dish I missed from home: banana leaves.

Truth be told, Filipino food made only occasional appearances in my kitchen; Italian dishes were the mainstay. It wasn't because I didn't miss the cuisine, because I did—a lot. It was because I was handicapped by the lack of ingredients. I could count on my fingers the Filipino dishes I cooked for my family. Among these, snagging top billing was my all-time favorite, inihaw na isda, or stuffed fish grilled in banana leaves. It is perhaps the simplest in the cuisine's repertoire. Aluminum foil could be used as a substitute wrapper as it cooked atop burning charcoal. But for me, banana leaves had no equal in bringing out the heart and soul of this dish.

Since I came from a big family of grilled-food lovers, inihaw reminded me of family get-togethers in the Philippines: an electric fan by the grill blowing smoke away from the house, chilled bottles of San Miguel beer clinking as they were passed around, and the fish's juices setting off a billowing cloud of smoke as they dripped onto the burning coals. As the banana leaves seared and the fish poached in its juices, the smoke imbued the air with faintly fruity and herbal scents. While the smell had the charm of an island paradise, the cottony white wisps were avoided at all costs. Everyone tried to dodge the smoke, especially from getting in their eyes, since it made them tear and sting.

Local Italian plant shops have since started stocking up on a bewildering range of exciting cultivars, including banana and calamansi plants in pots. I am currently a proud owner of a 10-foot-tall moringa tree, five little calamansi trees, and a growing banana tree. I use all of them in cooking my favorite Filipino dishes.

Gone are the long sleepless nights of Internet-hunting for tropical

Since I came from a big family of grilled-food lovers, inihaw reminded me of family get-togethers in the Philippines: an electric fan by the grill blowing smoke away from the house, chilled bottles of San Miguel beer clinking as they were passed around, and the fish's juices setting off a billowing cloud of smoke as they dripped onto the burning coals.

plants, weeks of waiting for seeds to show signs of life, and months or years of nursing and nurturing seedlings to see them grow past their critical stages. Call it an attempt to develop a cure for my bouts of homesickness or an attempt to manifest and perpetuate my identity on foreign soil, or perhaps part of my nesting and maternal instincts. I just know that one of the best ways to get living beings to thrive outside of their natural habitat is to recreate conditions closely resembling the environment of their genetic makeup. That holds true for me, my non-endemic plants, and my Italian-born children.

When I grill fish swathed in my garden-grown banana leaves, I notice how differently my two kids and I react to the smoke permeating the air. While a smile works its way across my face when the familiar aroma dances its way to my nostrils, my young ones wrinkle their noses, perplexed by the smell. I hope it's just a matter of time before their perplexity turns to delight.

With luck and patience, I relive my gastronomic memories right in my own kitchen in Italy with my husband and kids. Happiness billows when I see, smell, and taste the flavors of the islands and share with my kids what I had grown up loving in the country they barely know. Inevitably, smoke gets in my eyes in the process, but who cares? Smoke is the precursor to a delicious Filipino-inspired meal. ◆

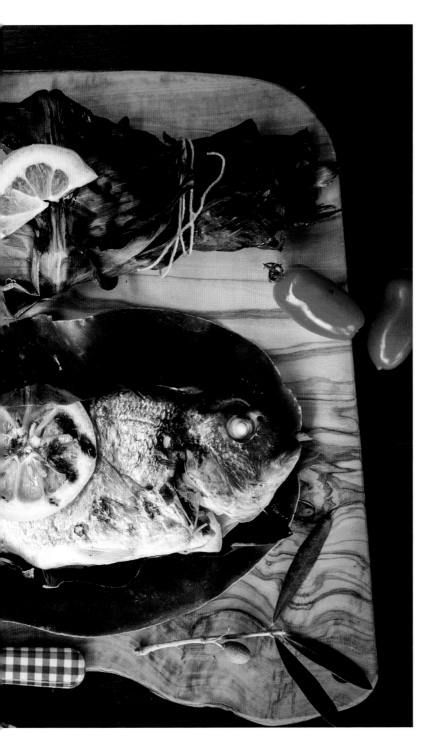

*< Inihaw na Isda at Ensaladang
Talong (page 36)*

INIHAW NA ISDA AT ENSALADANG TALONG

STUFFED FISH GRILLED IN BANANA LEAVES AND EGGPLANT SALAD WITH TOASTED PANCETTA

PREPARATION TIME: 45 minutes

YIELD: 2 servings

2 tomatoes, small diced

1 red onion, small diced

1 (2-inch) piece ginger, peeled and grated

2 (1-pound) whole white fish (such as sea bream), scaled, gutted, rinsed, and patted dry

4 thin lemon slices

Salt, to taste

2 large banana leaves, rinsed and dried

Eggplant Salad (recipe follows), for serving

Vanilla Rice (recipe follows), for serving

Prepare a charcoal grill.

In a bowl, mix together the tomatoes, onion, and ginger. Stuff the stomach of each fish with half of the tomato mixture. Add two slices of lemon to each. Season both sides of the fish with salt.

Place the banana leaves on a clean work surface. Place one stuffed fish on top of each leaf. Wrap each fish in a banana leaf and tie with kitchen twine, if needed, to close tightly (see Note).

Grill the fish packets for 10 to 15 minutes per side. To check for doneness, poke the fish with the tip of a knife. If the flesh is still translucent and sticks to the bone, close the packet and continue grilling. When cooked through, unwrap the fish, discard the banana leaves, and serve immediately with the eggplant salad and vanilla rice.

NOTE: The spine of the banana leaf can be removed and used as food string to secure the packet, if needed.

Wrapping food in banana leaves is a distinctive cooking method in Philippine cuisine. The leaves allow the food to poach in its own juice and lend a faint but delectable aroma of fruit and herbs to the dish. Heavenly aroma aside, I love how a mélange of flavors gets trapped inside the parcel and how it keeps the fish moist and tender. In the Philippines, bangus (milkfish) or tilapia is used in this recipe, but other kinds of white fish—like sea bream, sea bass, halibut, cod, and snapper—also work well.

When Filipinos eat grilled food, it's often paired with eggplant salad. The eggplant is charred until the skin is almost black (and ugly), but when you slice it open to scoop out the pulp, the smokiness can make you drool. This is a basic mix with onions, tomatoes, and vinegar. If you're feeling more adventurous, some versions add bagoong (shrimp paste), green mangoes, and salted duck eggs.

EGGPLANT SALAD

3 medium eggplants

1 tomato, small diced

½ red onion, small diced

2 tablespoons finely chopped fresh flat-leaf parsley

¼ cup vinegar of your choice

Salt and freshly ground black pepper, to taste

2 ounces pancetta, diced

Pierce the eggplants all over with a sharp knife. Place them on a hot grill or directly on the burner of a gas stove and turn them frequently until the skin is charred all over. Remove the eggplants from the heat, let them cool enough to touch them, then peel and discard the skin.

Transfer the eggplant pulp to a medium bowl, then break it apart using two forks. Add the tomato, onion, parsley, and vinegar, mixing well. Taste and add salt and pepper as needed. Set the eggplant mixture aside.

In a small saucepan, toast the pancetta over low heat for about 5 minutes, or until crunchy but not burned. Discard the fat. Add the pancetta to the eggplant salad. Serve at room temperature.

VANILLA RICE WITH TOASTED SESAME SEEDS

1½ cups long-grain rice

2¾ cups water

1 vanilla pod, halved lengthwise

2 tablespoons sesame seeds

Combine the rice, water, and vanilla pod in a medium saucepan and bring to a boil over medium-high heat. Reduce the heat to low. Cover the pan almost completely, leaving it just slightly uncovered, and simmer until the rice completely absorbs the water. While the rice is cooking, toast the sesame seeds in a small saucepan over low heat for about 3 minutes, or until the seeds turn brown.

When the rice is cooked, remove and discard the vanilla pod. Sprinkle the toasted sesame seeds on top. Serve warm or store in an airtight container in the refrigerator or freezer until ready to use.

THE HEAT IS ON
{AS TOLD TO THE EDITOR}

T HE STATE OF my body and mind is the antithesis of our serene out-door cook-off location: the topiary-hedged gardens of Napa Val-ley's Beringer Vineyards. Three of us cheftestants have made it through the first round of Food Network's *Chopped Grill Masters*. Before us loom char-black mystery baskets containing the ingredients we must fire up into a cohesive and impressive entrée.

"Are you ready to excel at the grill with whatever you find in these?" asks host Ted Allen, gesturing to the baskets.

I nod and force out a "Yeah." But who am I kidding? One of the grill masters I face off with is a James Beard Award–winning chef. What chance do I stand pitted against him? I am too tense to even stay fo-cused, let alone think and cook under pressure.

I open the two-lid wicker basket for the big reveal: a whole red snap-per, a jug of Meyer lemonade, a bundle of beets, and—for the curveball—a bunch of grape leaves. Right! Earthy and salty grape leaves! What in the world am I to do with those? Aside from using them to patch up a wound to stop the blood flow if I accidentally chop off my finger, nothing comes to mind.

"Thirty minutes is all you've got," Ted announces. "The clock starts now!"

The heat is on from the sweltering sun, the flames of the grills, and the intensity of the competition. I pull up the sleeves of my orange chef's jacket and scramble to the pantry. *What do I need?* I grab a box of brown sugar and a bottle of apple cider vinegar, thinking I will pickle the beets together with the Meyer lemonade. I grab a bottle of fish sauce

CHRISSY CAMBA is the co-chef/owner of Maddy's Dumpling House in Chicago. Shortly after graduating from Loyola University Chicago with a degree in biology, Chrissy fell in love with cooking. She was invited to stage in a restaurant kitchen, which later offered her her first kitchen job. After many accolades, a stint on Bravo TV's *Top Chef* season 10, and the passing of her bunny, Maddy, Chrissy started Maddy's Dumpling House as an homage to her beloved bunny. Currently, Maddy's Dumpling House pops up once a month around Chicago until a permanent brick-and-mortar space is found.

and a jar of chile-garlic sauce for a fish broth. *Hmmm . . . and what else? How can I make those grape leaves sizzle without overpowering the other ingredients?* A complete mental block. If Lola were watching, she'd be telling me off: "Have you not learned anything from me?"

Most of my childhood was spent in the kitchen cooking Filipino food with Lola. Now a nonagenarian, my grandmother has softened up—a lot. But back in my elementary and high school days, she was a firecracker. Strict. Stoic. Did I mention strict? My parents were divorced by the time I turned two, and my mother, a single parent, worked hard to provide the world for my brother and me. Since Mother worked so much, she brought a backup into our home in Chicago: my lola.

I watched and assisted Lola plenty of times in the kitchen. One of my most vivid memories is of her preparing my favorite Filipino dish—crab torta, or omelet. Prepping started the moment Lola was handed a bag of fresh live crabs. She had a meticulous nature about her, never cutting corners and never rushing. Everything was always timed perfectly.

Instead of steaming the crabs right off the bat, she first gave them a nice bath. She filled the just-cleaned kitchen sink halfway with water and released the crabs into it. I asked why. She said, "They are very sandy and need to be cleaned before they are cooked." It didn't make sense to me at the time because the exterior of the crabs looked clean to me. Once we took them out of the water, I realized that the washing was happening on the inside. The spongy gills that act as filters were caked with ocean sand. Soaking the crabs in fresh water induced them to purge the dirt.

One of my most vivid memories is of Lola preparing my favorite Filipino dish—crab torta, or omelet. She had a meticulous nature about her, never cutting corners and never rushing. Everything was always timed perfectly.

———

Cradling the ingredients I snatched from the pantry in my arms, I take a deep breath to expel the self-doubt that is blurring my brain. As I hurry back to my station, my confidence grows. I know exactly what to do—thank you, Lola.

Tempting as it is to throw the grape leaves over the coals as they are, I douse them first with Meyer lemonade in a bowl. I toss them into the acidic liquid to wash the salinity off them, like Lola washed the grit from the crabs.

With time rapidly vanishing, I perform a balancing act of multitasking: tending three pans of sauces simmering over the grill, chopping ingredients, and checking on the whole snapper sitting in the smoker to develop flavor.

I whiz to the smoker and lift the lid. Ta-da! A colossal plume of smoke soars into the air. I take out the fish—it's lightly cooked to my liking, but the final transformation is yet to come.

The dramatic smoke effect is reminiscent of the times Lola opened the crab steamer. She pulled the shellfish from the billowing steam as if she were pulling a rabbit out of a magic hat. But that was just the first act of the performance. While the crabs were still warm to the touch, Lola worked on the painstaking job of removing their shells. When all the crabmeat was taken out and the intact carapaces were emptied and set aside, the final act of cooking the torta began: sautéing, scrambling, stuffing, and pan-frying until the formerly inedible-looking creatures were reconstructed into their appetizing and easy-to-eat versions.

At some stage—around the point when Lola mixed the crabmeat with the beaten eggs—the desire for instant gratification always got the better of me. I felt frustrated and almost sad. I thought the crabmeat mixture, on its own, was already a delicious treat. Why bother combining and cooking it with eggs? Why wait a few moments longer? It was only when I saw and tasted the final blending of flavors and textures that I learned what taking food to the next level entailed—patience, discipline, and focus.

"Okay folks," Ted warns, "we have only five minutes left in this round!"

Yet the snapper still needs to go through its abracadabra transformation—calling on my knife and char-grilling skills. I'm in full-blown panic mode. I wipe the beads of sweat forming profusely on my forehead with the back of my hand and fillet the fish. As I fire it up on the grill, one of the judges yells, "C'mon guys, get it on the plate!" I can feel the judges' eyes on me. My hands shake as I plate my dish: lightly smoked red snapper in a chile–Meyer lemonade broth with charred pickled beets and grape leaves salad. The countdown from 10 to one starts.

"Time's up!"

My two competitors and I march down the aisle to the chopping block in single file. One of our dishes is about to face execution on worldwide TV. I can only sympathize with Marie Antoinette as she took her last steps to the guillotine in front of a crowd of spectators.

One dish sits on the chopping block. Ted raises the cloche. I can't believe it! It's not mine! I'm not chopped. Not yet. I'm advancing to the last round, where I will battle it out for a spot in the finale.

Whenever the heat is on—whether from family matters, such as the aftermath of my parents' divorce, from my demanding work as a chef, or from fierce challenges, like today's competition—Lola's influence never fails to turn down the flame to a manageable notch. I wish she were watching me now, as she usually did when I took the first bite of her golden-brown crusted crab torta, relishing in the joy she had given me. ◆

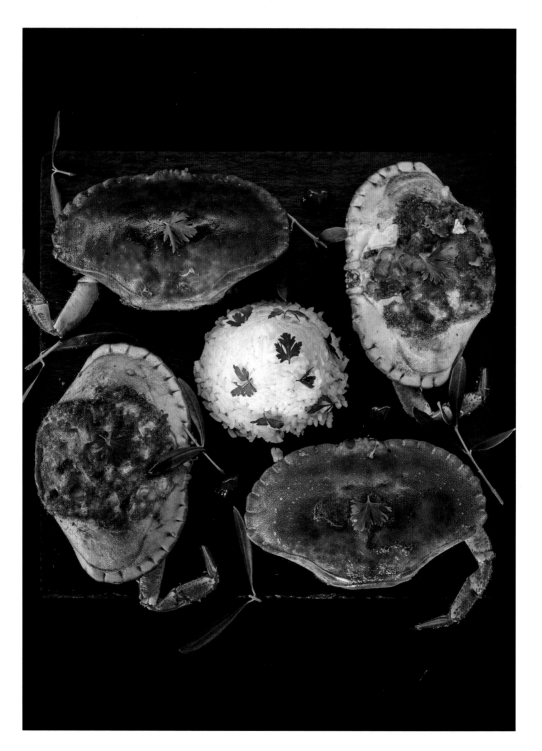

CRAB TORTA

CRAB OMELET

PREPARATION TIME: 1 hour + 2 hours to soak and shell the crabs

YIELD: 10 servings

The word torta *has different culinary meanings in Philippine cuisine. There is a sweet* torta, *which is a type of cake in the Visayas region, and then there's the nationally known savory* torta, *which refers to a variety of omelet dishes. It's tempting to cut corners with this dish, but to do it justice, you must have patience.*

10 live crabs (preferably blue crabs)

Fine salt, to taste

Canola oil, for cooking

2 tablespoons minced garlic

1 medium yellow onion, small diced

5 Yukon gold potatoes, peeled and small diced

5–6 large eggs

Freshly ground black pepper, to taste

10 cups steamed rice, for serving

To steam the crabs, fill a clean kitchen sink halfway with cold tap water. Add the live crabs and allow them to swim for 1 hour. Be careful, as the crabs will pinch if you get too close.

Pour 1 inch of water into a large stockpot. Add a generous pinch of salt and the crabs. Cover and steam over medium-high heat for about 10 minutes, or until the shells turn reddish orange. Using a pair of tongs, remove the crabs from the pot, place on a tray or platter, and allow to cool to the touch.

To shell each crab, twist and pull the big front claws from the body and set aside. Peel off the flap of shell on the crab's underside (the abdomen) and discard. Detach the back shell (the carapace) from the body by anchoring your thumbs into the hole where the abdomen was. Remove and discard the innards from the carapace and set the shell aside. Remove the soft, pointy gills from the body and discard. Snap the body in half and pick out the meat. Put the meat in a large bowl. Crack the legs and claws using a mallet or nutcracker. Pick out the meat, add it to the bowl, and set aside.

To make the omelet, pour enough oil into a large nonstick skillet to coat the bottom. Add the garlic and onion and cook over medium-high heat until the onion is translucent, about 5 minutes. With a slotted spoon, transfer the onion and garlic to a plate and set it aside. Leave the excess oil in the pan.

Recipe continues >

Add more oil to the pan to coat the bottom and raise the heat to high. Carefully add the potatoes and season with salt. Pan-fry until the potatoes are golden brown on all sides, about 10 minutes. Transfer the potatoes to paper towels to drain.

Add the cooked onion, garlic, and potatoes to the bowl of crabmeat and mix well. Taste and add salt as needed.

Crack the eggs into a bowl and season with about ¼ teaspoon each of salt and pepper. Whisk thoroughly to combine. Add the eggs to the crab mixture and mix to combine.

Stuff the egg and crab mixture into the reserved shells and place them, open sides up, on a platter. If you have extra filling, set it aside.

To cook the omelet, pour enough oil into a large nonstick pan to cover the bottom. Heat the oil over medium-high heat until it shimmers. Gently add the stuffed shells to the pan, open sides down, making sure to turn them into the oil away from you to prevent the hot oil from splashing back at you. Cook for 3 to 5 minutes, until the stuffed shells can be lifted without the insides falling out, and then turn the shells onto the other side and cook for 3 minutes. Transfer the shells to a serving plate.

Any excess filling can be cooked in the pan for about 3 minutes, or until it looks like a thin, lacy-edged pancake. Serve the torta and extra filling with rice.

ANG PAMBIHIRANG LUTO NI NANAY

{MOM'S EXTRAORDINARY COOKING}

CRISTETA "CRIS" COMERFORD was born in Manila, Philippines. After serving as an assistant chef in the White House during the Clinton administration, in 2005 she was appointed by First Lady Laura Bush to executive chef, a position she still holds. Cris is the first woman and first minority to hold the position since the Kennedys created the position in 1961. Outside of the White House, she has served as a church deacon and currently leads a home study group with her husband, John. They have both volunteered for humanitarian trips to an impoverished town in Brazil. Cris lives with her family in Columbia, Maryland, in between visiting family in Seattle and Chicago.

MY ELDEST SISTER, Flor, was a public-school teacher in Manila when she sent my daughter, Danielle, a wonderful collection of Filipino children's fiction books. One peculiar story, *Ang Pambihirang Buhok ni Raquel* (*Raquel's Extraordinary Hair*) by Luis Gatmaitan, was about a city girl named Raquel, who was greatly envied by her cousin for many reasons. She had outward beauty, flawless skin, and the most unusual and stunning multicolored hair. But Raquel's most important attribute was her positive and encouraging influence on her cousin. Despite seeming so perfect in so many ways, Raquel had something unknown to all. She had leukemia. And yet Raquel never let her disease overshadow her perspective on life. She was contagiously uplifting to those around her.

My nanay (mother), Erlinda, or Nana Pate, as she was fondly called by all, exuded a similar confidence and tenacity. Nana Pate was known throughout our neighborhood, especially for her extraordinary culinary skills and abilities. But her giftedness extended beyond cooking—she also ran a dress shop in our house. Growing up, I usually came home to a house full of seamstresses and dressmakers, young and old ladies with their patterns and fabrics doing fittings and finishings. Elegant dresses were displayed throughout our home.

She ran her dress shop as any other CEO would run a great company, yet she never forgot that the most important tool in her life was not her Singer sewing machine, but rather her propane-powered stove.

In between serving her dress shop clientele, she took care of feeding a family of a dozen or more, depending on how many extended family members stopped by at any given time. Many Filipino families are so close-knit that even a third cousin is as important as the first. Nanay's language of love was cooking, and I had the blessing of growing up around the most talented and most efficient "chef." Many well-known chefs will tell you that their earliest and greatest influence was their mom. My mom was indeed the best cook I knew. No matter how busy her dress shop became or what life handed her, she made sure that she always took time to cook for the people she loved the most.

Nanay, like Raquel in the book, impressed everyone with her beautiful dresses and memorable and delicious meals. But it was the spirit in which she gave that no one will ever forget. Her recipes, though so well known, were not written, but engraved in everyone's heart.

Escabeche, a sweet-and-sour marinated fish dish, is one of those recipes that Mom cooked only on very special occasions. It required some advance preparations and fish butchery, something she was always very happy to do. In her memory, I am honored to share this family recipe, so enjoyed and so remembered by all those whose lives she touched. ◆

Left to right: Nanay with Cris in the White House kitchen; Cris's nanay and Cris's daughter

ESCABECHE-INSPIRED FRIED SNAPPER

PREPARATION TIME: 30 minutes

YIELD: 2 servings

Escabeche is a traditional Spanish dish that involves marinating a protein (commonly fish, pork, chicken, or rabbit in Spain) in an acid, such as vinegar. Versions of this dish are popular in other European and Latin American countries with Spanish influence. The Philippines was a colony of Spain from 1521 to 1898, so it's not surprising that we took this dish and put our own spin on it. In this recipe, the fish is not marinated, but rather drizzled with a sauce made of vinegar and sweet-and-sour orange juice.

FISH

Canola oil, for frying

1 (2-pound) whole red snapper, black sea bass, or similar fish, cleaned and scaled

Kosher salt, to taste

2 cups Wondra flour

SAUCE

½ cup rice vinegar

½ cup banana ketchup

¼ cup turbinado sugar

Grated zest and juice of 1 orange

1 tablespoon orange marmalade

1½ tablespoons cornstarch

VEGETABLES

1 tablespoon olive oil

1 red onion, thinly sliced

6 cloves garlic, sliced

1 (1-inch) piece fresh ginger, peeled and thinly sliced

1 red bell pepper, seeded and thinly sliced

1 banana pepper, thinly sliced

SERVING

2 scallions, cut lengthwise into thin strips, for garnish

3 sprigs cilantro, for garnish

2 cups cooked jasmine rice, for serving

Make the fish: Pour enough oil into a large wok or deep frying pan to submerge the whole fish. Heat the oil over high heat until a deep-fry thermometer reads 375°F.

Recipe continues >

ESCABECHE–INSPIRED FRIED SNAPPER

continued

Generously season the fish inside and out with salt. Pour the flour onto a platter and dredge the fish in it, shaking off the excess. Carefully lower the whole fish into the oil and cook, without moving it, for 12 to 15 minutes, until the fish is crisped and golden brown. Transfer the fried fish to a wire rack or paper towels to drain.

Make the sauce: While the fish is cooking, whisk together all the sauce ingredients in a small saucepot set over medium heat. Cook, whisking constantly, until the mixture has thickened. Remove the sauce from the heat and set it aside.

Make the vegetables: Heat the oil in a medium sauté pan over medium-high heat until it shimmers. Add the onion, garlic, ginger, and peppers and cook, stirring occasionally, for 2 to 3 minutes, until the vegetables soften slightly but remain crisp.

To serve, set the fish in the center of a large platter and drizzle it with the sauce. Top the fish with the vegetables and garnish with the scallions and cilantro. Serve with the jasmine rice.

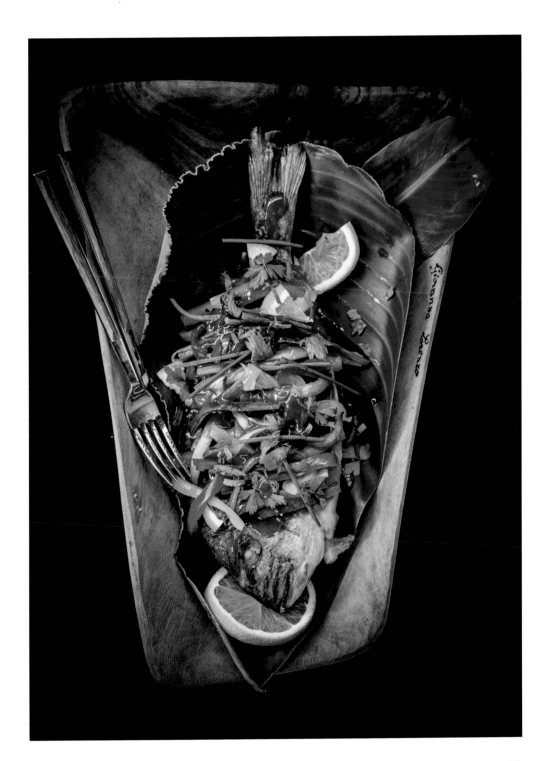

CHAPTER 2
POULTRY

HERE ARE FOUR different ways to cook chicken: the classic adobo method of marinating and braising with vinegar, a modern sous vide deep-fried chicken, a simmered chicken-soup-for-the-soul tinola, and the Spanish-influenced tomato-based stew called afritada. This chapter's adobo recipe is what is known in the Philippines as adobo sa gata or ginataang adobo, a hybrid between adobo and ginataan, the term for cooking with coconut milk. Infusing coconut milk in dishes is a popular culinary practice in Southern Luzon.

Philippine cuisine sits well with the growing movement of utilizing food scraps to reduce waste. While the recipes here call for thighs, breast, or wings, all parts of the chicken—including cuts often thrown away, such as heads, feet, necks, and offal—have always been welcomed in Philippine cooking.

EIGHT WAYS TO COOK LIKE MA

"WE CAME HERE BECAUSE WE WERE HUNGRY."

—Dr. Dawn Mabalon, historian, food scholar, and author of Little Manila Is in the Heart

1.   FOR MUCH LONGER than she's known me, my mom has been cooking to save lives in my family. My mother is the youngest daughter of seven children, just as I am the youngest daughter in my family among my cousins on her side. I place myself within this matrilineal stronghold because it's what has fed me. I visit her at her house—where I say I mostly grew up—at least once a week, or every two weeks, or when it's the end of the month and I'm broke from trying to be the responsible adult she needs me to be. This past weekend's visit was no different than previous ones: she wanted to talk about money, we enjoyed each other's company watching The Filipino Channel, we talked about Philippine President Rodrigo Duterte, she cooked tinola (chicken soup) from scratch for me, and we ate. It was love, and chicken, and home.

2.   When my cousins immigrated to the United States from Umingan, Pangasinan, Philippines, Ma commented on the amount of food they placed on their white plastic plates (you know, the ones that come in bulk from Costco). The food amounted to a small dome, a good two or three layers of various dishes atop their white rice. Ma will forever deny this, but I swear she said, "That's how you know they're new here. Your uncles Danny and Aries did the same thing when they came." She meant no shame nor shaming. "They were so skinny before! I'll find the pictures," she said. "You'll see." Ma turns her shit-talking into charm—a skill I'm still developing.

JANICE LOBO SAPIGAO is a writer, poet, and educator from San Jose, California. She was named one of the San Francisco Bay Area's 2017 Women to Watch by KQED Arts. She is also the author of *like a solid to a shadow* and her first book of poetry, *microchips for millions*. She is a VONA/Voices Fellow and Kundiman Poetry Fellow. Janice earned a BA with honors in ethnic studies from UC San Diego and an MFA in writing from CalArts.

3.   When we were younger, my brother, William, cousin Richard, and I stayed full from the many products bought at Costco. Everything at Costco—beef- and shrimp-flavored Cup Noodles, beef- and chicken-flavored ramen, microwaveable teriyaki bowls, Nestlé Drumstick 16-count variety packs—is my nostalgia. A lot of our classmates growing up might have had these meals at home, or in their lunch pails, too. Cheap or free Costco food made us devious. One time my grandma Concepcion and I were trying to get in the store to meet family members inside without our family's Costco card—so we walked in behind another Filipino family, and none of the workers noticed, nor did the family say anything. She will deny this, too, but Ma loved the samples of their fish nuggets, but they were too expensive and therefore unjustifiable to purchase in bulk. So she sent my brother and me back and forth to the free samples booth at least 10 times total. We worried we'd get caught, but I realized that I was small enough to hide behind crowds and the booth's microwave, and I had a wingspan long enough to reach around the microwave to scoop a free sample or two for Ma. Costco brings a joy akin to the satisfaction of a good meal to immigrant and working-class families.

4.   When I was in graduate school in Los Angeles, I cooked Ma's tinola for the first time. At least once a month for two years, I'd cook this dish to make, build, recreate, and taste the home I'd left. Ma's recipe is, like Costco, economical. Oil in a saucepan. Sautéed garlic, onions, and ginger

(if I have it). The smell from this mixture alone transports me back to San Jose, to Ma's kitchen, to my childhood. Salt and pepper the chicken. After a few minutes, add the chicken (my family uses chicken wings). Cook until they brown. Add water. Let the gang simmer to a boil. You can add chayote. Some greens. You can add papaya. More salt and pepper to taste. I like my tinola like Ma: simple.

5.　In college, I first learned how to cook for myself when my friend Liezl, her boyfriend, and I were craving Spam. We walked (or hiked, rather) to a campus grocery store and spent our meal points on a very expensive single can of Spam, eggs, and rice. We walked back to my dormitory's communal kitchen and started prepping. We talked about how we liked our Spam slices either super crispy, or thin, or thick, and whether we liked the end or middle pieces. We ate all eight dollars of it, I think. We might have eaten all 10 dollars of our rice, too.

6.　I was always quiet in school until high school, and teachers liked that. My third-grade teacher, Ms. Jackson, once asked me loudly, "So, you speak Ill-low-kah?" I didn't know what she meant. "You speak Ill-low-kah, at home?" The *ka* sounded more and more like a caged bird trying to get out with each repetition. I tried to match her word with what I knew, her half pronunciation of Ilokano[1] still not registering with me, and stayed quiet. So did she. "Um. Yes," I said, to break the awkward silence.

"Good!" she said. "Do your homework and practice your language for an hour every day."

Thankfully, my mom appeared in our classroom soon after, and she saved me from this moment of premature othering. I didn't know I was Ilokano. Someone said something to me in Tagalog and I slow-blinked back at them, waiting for my mind to match their words with my memories. Nothing. It wasn't like when someone spoke to me in Spanish, since I could match their words with words in Ilokano so that I could halfway understand.

1　Ilokano, or Ilocano, is one of the largest ethnolinguistic groups in the Philippines.

Ma's recipe is, like Costco, economical. Oil in a saucepan. Sautéed garlic, onions, and ginger (if I have it). The smell from this mixture alone transports me back to San Jose, to Ma's kitchen, to my childhood.

7. In my first semester in college in San Diego, I called Ma from one of the processed foods aisles at Ralph's in La Jolla. I asked her for some of the basic ingredients I'd needed to cook tinola, for when the weekend came. I hadn't been eating too well, or at all, and I found myself getting sick often. I was also sad and homesick, trying my best to find friends, missing my boyfriend, and hungry for home. I'd often stay in my dorm room eating handfuls of Kix cereal instead of walking half a mile to the nearest (and the tiniest!) cafeteria. I wanted that recipe. So, when I asked my mom for it, she said, "Janice, it's 10 o'clock on a Tuesday. Why are you grocery shopping at night?" She was right. I left the grocery store empty-handed.

8. I cook now for me and my partner on Mondays and Wednesdays. We take turns because our lives are so busy, and we've divided up days, meals, and chores, so that we can better manage our time together as well as taking care of each other. When I cook tinola or adobo (Ma taught me that I could easily turn tinola into adobo), I imagine—and I didn't before—cooking this meal for my children. I imagine telling them these stories of people whom they may never meet.

When I was 15, I didn't know how to act around little kids. When I was 18, I naively told Ma that I didn't want kids. When I was 21, I absolutely did not want kids. When I was 24, I lost faith in ever meeting anyone worthy of having kids with. Now, I am 29, and I love kids. I dream (or, romanticize, rather) of cooking for and loving them the way Ma did for me and my brother. Food is futuristic and legendary this way. ◆

TINOLA

Tinola's simplicity makes it a classic Filipino soul food—humble, soothing, and reminiscent of warm memories of family dinners. This beloved indigenous dish even makes an appearance in one of the greatest Filipino classic novels, Noli Me Tángere, which was published in 1887. In the chapter titled "Hapunan" ("Dinner"), chicken tinola was the welcome-home dish served at a banquet for the lead character, Crisóstomo Ibarra, upon his return to the motherland after having spent almost seven years abroad. At the table, antagonist Padre Dámaso felt offended when he saw that the plate dished out to him contained the scrappiest parts of the chicken (the neck and wings), while others got thighs and breasts. No one's getting offended here. Everyone gets wings! Besides, the wings' cartilage and collagen add oodles of flavor to the soup.

PREPARATION TIME: 30 minutes + 1 hour to simmer
YIELD: 6 servings

3 pounds chicken wings, cut at the joints (remove skin if you prefer a low-fat soup)

Salt and freshly ground black pepper, to taste

2 tablespoons cooking oil

3 cloves garlic, minced

1 onion, sliced

1 (2-inch) piece fresh ginger, peeled and minced

2–3 small or medium chayotes or green papayas, peeled, seeded, and cubed (optional)

1 cup moringa leaves, chile leaves, or chopped bok choy

Season the chicken all over with salt and pepper. Set aside.

In a medium stockpot, heat the oil over medium heat until it shimmers. Add the garlic, onion, and ginger. Cook for 3 to 4 minutes, until the onion is softened.

Add the chicken and cook until light brown, about 2 minutes on each side. Add enough water to the pot to cover all the ingredients and bring to a boil. Reduce the heat to low, cover, and simmer for 1 hour.

Add the chayotes, if using. Cover and continue to simmer until soft, about 5 minutes. Add the moringa. Cover and cook for a few seconds. Remove from the heat and serve hot.

NOTE: If you kept the chicken skin on and find the soup too greasy, strain the broth into a jar or other narrow vessel, such as a water pitcher. The grease will rise to the top as the soup cools. Skim the grease off with a chilled spoon or use a baster. Pour the soup back into the pot and bring to a boil.

IN THE GREAT WHITE NORTH

T HIRTY SECONDS—that's all it took for my spit to turn to ice. After watching my saliva solidify, my eight-year-old, brown-eyed, brown-skinned chubby self hurried off to school. Luckily, school was just less than half a mile from where we lived. Because I lunched at home, I nipped over this path four times a day, under any weather condition, except for one: a wind chill. On days when wind chill warnings were issued, the wind could huff temperatures down to a frostbiting –40°F. Of course, my parents wouldn't let us out unless our bodies were securely swaddled with layers of garments and our extremities were entirely shielded by knit hats, gloves of fur and leather, and snow boots.

Getting dressed for a wind chill took at least 15 minutes. Once completely covered and almost suffocated with warmth, I was raring to go. As soon as I opened the door, a burst of air hit my face and the howling of the wind greeted me. The usual five- to 10-minute walk to school could turn into a 40-minute trek.

The trek presented hurdles, such as snowdrifts of up to 10 feet, which seemed as challenging to scale as Mount Everest. Each step on the soft snow swallowed my leg up to the knee. The demon, as I liked to call the wind chill, was just that. When nature turned into a monster, you could feel the cold piercing all the way to the bone. When it reared its ugly head, it felt like jagged ice shards ripped into your face, which eventually led to a numbing nothingness.

The bright side was, during a wind chill advisory, my treks between school and home were reduced from four to two; instead of going home

for lunch, I stayed at school, happy to take a packed lunch Mom prepared in the early morning.

The first time I ate lunch at school, my eyes nearly popped out of my head. It was like the clouds opened up and—BOOM!—a light from the gods shone down and revealed all the treasures of the world. There at the dining hall glowed mini tabletop video arcade games of Pac-Man and Galaga, handheld football video games, Connect Four, Hungry Hippos—you name it, they had it. It was a boy's paradise, especially a Filipino immigrant boy like me whose parents struggled to make ends meet.

After gawking at all the toys, I sat at the lunch table with the other kids. We set our lunches down and started unpacking our bounties. One kid had Alpha-Getti, a canned childhood delight of pasta and tomato sauce, and it was hot to boot inside a thermos that came with its own spoon. Others had sandwiches galore: ham and cheese, tuna, egg salad, and peanut butter and jam, mmm. I loved peanut butter and jam, but we hardly ate it at home. More common were sweet red sausages (longganisa), fried salty fish (tuyo), and fried meat with fried eggs and garlic fried rice.

I reached into the brown paper containing my packed lunch, or baon. A metallic, cold-to-the-touch wrapping rustled as I gripped it with my fingers. I pulled it out of the bag and set it on the table. I looked at it for a moment, knowing that whatever was inside had to be eaten without utensils and cold. There was only one microwave at the lunch hall, and it was busy churning out some kid's soup or some rich kid's Pizza Pops.

Although ALLAN PINEDA officially earned his culinary arts diploma in 2005, he's been in the culinary industry for more than 22 years. Alongside his wife, Amanda, Allan is the cofounder of Manila Nights, a Filipino-inspired pop-up dinner series in Winnipeg, Canada. He and Amanda were finalists for *Western Living*'s 2017 Foodies of the Year award. The dynamic duo has traveled to various cities worldwide, including San Francisco, London, and Sydney, to share their dishes. One may call Allan an ambassador of Filipino food for his drive toward spreading the cuisine and all its glory. After attending Savor Filipino, a food event in California, he became the social media coordinator of the Filipino Food Movement-Canada. He is the founder of Kitchen Kumite, a large-scale *Iron Chef*-style tournament, the proceeds of which go to cancer-care organizations.

And even at that age, I knew that aluminum foil in a microwave was a no-no. I could go home and endure the arctic weather outside, but without latticed snowshoes, there was no way I could make it home and back to school on time.

"Gurgle, gurgle," called my belly. The noise from my stomach told me I had no choice. It was time to eat. I unwrapped my lunch—fried chicken and rice! All hopes and dreams for sandwiches were smashed to smithereens. So, there I was, utensil-less, with my fried chicken and rice and a bunch of onlookers. Kids peered at me, spoons halfway to their open mouths, and paused to watch.

Back then, at my house, we sometimes ate with our hands, kamayan style, and chicken and rice was no exception. My dad, with his right foot and knee planted on the chair supporting his right upper arm, dangled his eating hand over the food. He rocked it old-school. He rarely used a spoon unless the food was nilaga, sinigang, or any other soup dish.

At the school's lunch table, with my cold fried chicken and cold rice, in cold foil with no cutlery, I couldn't make myself any smaller. Hunched over, trying to hide my weird lunch, I gathered all my strength to force my hands to do my bidding. Hunger overcame shame. I grabbed the chicken like a beast with one hand and took a savage bite. I put the chicken down, and with mechanical precision, my fingers masterfully collected some rice into a neat ball to shovel in my mouth. There was silence. It was like a scene from the *Nintendo Power* cartoons that had been paused: kids watching a Filipino boy eating with his hands.

This happened in the '80s. There was no Food Network, and TV channels were changed using a dial. There was not much multiculturalism then. Eating by hand, except for finger foods, was considered bizarre and practiced only by certain minority groups.

I finished my chicken and rice. It was a moment of awakening. I noticed how different I was from most others. Things started to make sense: why I had to take a Filipino class to learn the Filipino language as well as an ESL (English as a second language) class, even though I spoke English. And also, the crayons. Before then, I always used a pale peach-beige color when coloring people's skin in my drawings. It seemed standard practice. It hadn't occurred to me until then that there was, indeed, a wide variety of skin tones.

I am now an adult. It's been a year since I developed my own fried chicken recipe, and yet it still excites me every time I make it. I cook it first sous vide, a cooking technique that involves sealing the chicken in a bag and cooking it in a temperature-controlled water bath.

"So, is this fried chicken better for you?" my wife once asked.

"Hmmm . . . yeah. I think," I said. "Frying time is less, so it sits less in oil. The chicken is already cooked from the sous vide."

Healthier or not, the chicken is on point. There's something about the sous vide process that keeps in the moisture and flavor better than other cooking methods. The chicken develops a perfect crunch without all the grease of regular frying.

I was against sous vide cooking in my younger years and just bought a machine a few years ago. Maybe I was afraid of change, or maybe I was afraid to be different. Whichever the case, I'll take this golden-brown fried chicken over a peanut butter sandwich any day, just the way it is. ◆

SOUS VIDE FRIED CHICKEN BREASTS

PREPARATION TIME: 15 minutes + 1 hour to sous vide
YIELD: 4 servings

4 (6-ounce) boneless, skinless chicken breasts, rinsed, patted dry, and quartered

1 ¼ teaspoons fine sea salt, divided, plus more to taste

½ teaspoon freshly ground black pepper, plus more to taste

2 quarts canola oil

1 cup pastry or all-purpose flour

¾ teaspoon paprika

¾ teaspoon onion powder

¼ teaspoon garlic powder

2 cups buttermilk

Fried chicken may not seem very Filipino, but it is omnipresent in the Filipino diet. The dish is so integrated into the country's menu that Max's Restaurant, the iconic Philippine chain (also known as "the house that fried chicken built"), had been feeding Filipinos its version of fried chicken for years before KFC opened its first store.

More than the way it's prepared, what makes fried chicken Filipino is the way it is eaten—with rice. This recipe melds new-age cooking with an age-old family recipe. The sous vide method decreases frying time by more than 75 percent, which makes for very juicy chicken. If you don't have a sous vide machine, try the alternative method on the following page.

Heat enough water to immerse a sous vide bag with chicken breasts in a sous vide machine set to 155°F.

Season each side of the chicken pieces with 1 teaspoon of the salt and the pepper. Place them in a sous vide bag in a uniform layer and vacuum seal. Alternatively, use a zip-top freezer bag and press all the air out by flattening the bag before sealing it.

Place the bag in the sous vide water and let cook for 1 hour.

Remove the cooked chicken from the bag and place on a plate lined with paper towels. Pat the chicken dry on both sides.

In a deep fryer or large pot set over high heat, heat the oil until a deep-fry thermometer reads 400°F.

To make the coating, whisk together the flour, paprika, onion powder, garlic powder, and remaining ¼ teaspoon salt in a bowl. Pour the buttermilk into a separate bowl. Submerge the chicken pieces in the buttermilk and let them sit for 20 seconds. Remove the chicken pieces and dredge them in the flour mixture.

Working in batches so as not to overcrowd the pot, carefully drop the chicken pieces into the oil and fry for 2 to 3 minutes, until the chicken is golden brown; keep in mind that the chicken is already cooked from the sous vide process, so be careful not to overcook.

Using a strainer or tongs, transfer the chicken to a rack or paper towels to drain. Season with salt and pepper and serve.

SOUS VIDE ALTERNATIVE: Fill a large pot three-quarters of the way with water. Clamp a thermometer to the pot. If you do not have a clamp, periodically check the temperature of the water bath using a regular thermometer. Heat the water to 155°F. Place the chicken in a zip-top bag, press out all the air, and seal. Place the bag in the water and let cook for one hour. Maintain the temperature of the water bath at 155°F by adjusting the burner. If it gets too hot, remove some of the water from the pot and replace it with cooler water. Proceed with the recipe as written.

TO MAKE A HOME

MY LOLA WAS my mother—my chosen mom after Mercy, my birth mother, left when I was two or three years old. Mercy always said my grandmother would raise me better than she ever could; although she moved just a few blocks down from us in Carson, she rarely came around, missed all the birthday parties, first days of school, my first menstruation, my first everything.

My lola Pacita—Mama, as I called her—was the woman who taught me everything there was in being a woman. She was born in a coastal village off the shore of the South China Sea in the Philippines. She was the second eldest, an aristocratic daughter of the mayor in Aringay, La Union. Her father, my great-grandfather, Isidro Dulay Sr., owned a large cigar factory and employed the whole town during my lola's youth. Her sisters still joked that she made up the term "fashionably late"; every Sunday during mass, she would arrive half an hour late and walk down the center aisle with her heels clicking, interrupting the priest's sermon. She wore long, butterfly-style dresses sewed by her younger sisters and golden earrings and rings, her hair immaculate with that Imelda Marcos bump, eyes kohled and beckoning. Before she turned 20, she returned home after her big move to Manila, where she graduated from the Philippine Normal School to become a teacher. It was 1940, just a year before World War II broke out across the country and fighter jets bloodied the skies.

Mama survived the war, but not without being captured by the Japanese soldiers and held in a garrison for three months. When her father wanted her to marry a Chinese mestizo from another aristocratic

MELISSA R. SIPIN was born and raised in Carson, California. She teaches at California State University, Monterey Bay, in the social action and creative writing program. Her work has won *Glimmer Train*'s Fiction Open and the *Washington Square Review*'s Flash Fiction Award. She co-edited *Kuwento: Lost Things* and is editor in chief of *TAYO Literary Magazine*. Her work has been published by *Guernica* magazine, *VIDA: Women in Literary Arts*, *Eleven Eleven* journal, and the PEN American Center, among others. Melissa's fiction has won scholarships and fellowships from the MacDowell Colony, Poets & Writers, Vermont Studio Center, Kundiman Fiction Retreat, VONA/Voices Conference, Community of Writers at Squaw Valley, and Sewanee Writers' Conference. She is hard at work on a short story collection and novel.

familia, Mama chose to elope instead with a US-Philippine Army officer turned guerrilla—my grandfather—who died before I was born. My grandfather's heroic status from the war made my familia an easy target for Ferdinand Marcos when he came to power after the United States granted the Philippines its independence. Marcos claimed to be the "most decorated war hero of the country," and our family became poor because my grandfather refused to lie about his faux war medals. Marcos stripped my grandfather of his retirement and his rank, and we were thrust into poverty, especially since my great-grandfather's cigar factory and the mansion that my grandmother grew up in were burned during the war.

But Mama was the matriarch of the family. When her daughter, Auntie Lodie, married a US sailor in the 1960s, she convinced her to apply for her visa to the United States. When Mama finally arrived in California, she fought and paid to petition for every one of her children and siblings to come to America. During the late '70s and '80s, she worked in the tuna canneries, where her lungs filled with the fog of the San Pedro harbor, to make sure that everyone had something to eat on the table.

Mercy was right. Mama taught me everything: how to dress, draw my eyebrows, pencil in my lips, articulate, sit up straight and like a lady, cross my legs, command a room, distract a stranger if he insulted me, laugh, make friends, debate, trust my intellect, fight for my intellect. Mama was always my champion—the first one to tell anyone off, even if he was the principal of my middle school. The story is this: my father abruptly took me out of sixth grade and flew me halfway across the world to Manila, where I stayed for the next three months. My sister and I were supposed to be there for only a week, for my aunt's funeral. I missed the rest of sixth grade. When I returned, my teacher wanted me to repeat the year. Mama would not have it—she marched into the principal's office, pointed her finger, and shouted: "You will not put my daughter in sixth grade; my daughter is too smart; you see, my friend, my daughter is too smart. You are my friend, yes? Don't push Melissa back a grade."

The only thing Mama did not teach me was how to cook.

She was renowned among my family for being the best cook, the only cook, a maestro in the kitchen. Even Mercy, when she was still in our lives, had adored her cooking. Mercy once said that the only thing she couldn't beat was Mama's chicken adobo, something I sought so desperately to learn from her when I was child. But Mama was a hawk, a falcon, a lone wolf in the kitchen. Every dish was her secret recipe, every dish an artistic expression she made with her bare hands.

When I was a child, Mama tilled an Eden on Dolores Street, the one house I remember fondly from those turbulent times. Before I had reached the age of 12, I must have moved to over eight apartments or houses, living with this or that relative, this or that aunt, this or that uncle. It was Mama who made sure we had, at least, a roof over our heads. When we did have a house, a beautiful mission-style home on Dolores, she made a garden out of pink flowers, rooting and placing them all in the fountain out front, where an ivory wooden veranda enclosed the baby angel that stood at the epicenter. A wall of cacti lined the right side of the house. She would cut off the fleshy bits of the cacti and make a delicious dessert out of them with milk, sugar, and chopped avocados. She watered the mango and avocado trees with precision, every morning and every sunset.

Every day after school, I came home, walked into the yellow-tiled kitchen, and asked Mama, "Would you teach me how to cook Filipino food?"

She would smile out of disbelief that I thought she was willing to let anyone else into this cooking world of hers, a private space she kept hidden even from her two daughters and eight sons. She never wrote down recipes, always cooked by eyeing the soy sauce and vinegar, tasting the sauce before serving, and always said, "The saltier, the better, anak," the Filipino word for *child*.

Every time, it seemed that she would begin to teach me how to cook by placing ingredients on the bamboo cutting board and saying, "Feel the bay leaves. Touch the chile pepper. Smell the garlic." All from the garden she tilled out front. But that was as far as it went. When it got to stirring the sauce, or frying the onions and garlic, or cutting up the chiles, she would smack my hand away, shoo me off with her arms, and tell me, "Get out of my kitchen or else, bahala na," warning me that anything could happen.

I didn't learn how to cook until I was very far away from her, when I, too, had eloped with a US sailor. We both had our reasons to marry into the military, and it was always about survival.

Back then, when I created a recipe for my own chicken adobo, I was living in Charleston, South Carolina, 1500 miles away from Los Angeles, 1500 miles away from the place where Mama raised me. There was no Chinese, Filipino, Thai, or Indian restaurant for miles. My husband and I had to make do with the right ingredients from the commissary, where there was at least an aisle for Filipino ingredients, like Datu Puti vinegar.

Mama, by then, had already passed. She was buried deep within the hills between San Pedro and Palos Verdes, submerged in the earth with my grandfather, the war hero she had loved deeply before my time.

One day at the commissary, there was a lola who walked very slowly, holding her grandson, pointing at different products and naming them aloud. I sighed, and the lola turned to me to apologize, to excuse her slowness. I shook my head, said, "No, no, I just miss my lola." She said, "Ah, anak, where is she now? Here? Home in the Philippines?" I said, "No, Lola, she has passed on." She gave me that sad, sad meaningful look Mama would give me, the face she used as she'd point to everyone in the store and say, "You see there? He is my friend, my good friend!" That face of longing, like she was judging the world intently.

I could see the lola hold her grandson's hand a little tighter. She asked me where she passed, and I said California. She repeated the word the same way Mama would, the right pitch, accent, and sadness. "Oh, California? Not home?"

The day I learned how to cook, the day I learned to make my own chicken adobo, just the way Mama would have loved it, I was alone. My husband was away at duty that night, like most nights while he was still in the navy, and I was thinking of Mama. I always am. It's in the way I pick out fruits, touch basil or bay leaves, peer at them and hold each one in my hand firmly as if I were judging the world. It's the way I look at every Filipino in the grocery store and think: that person, they're my friend. And because I missed her so, I willed this chicken adobo out of me.

My first step was calling my father to ask how my grandmother made his favorite dish. He barely remembered, but he at least remembered the ingredients, which is all I really needed. My father's fractured memory helped me create my own chicken adobo, made in my own secret recipe, in my own private world—something, I know, Mama would be proud of. She taught me everything. (Everything but how to cook!) But the most important gift she left me was this: to take whatever I had, whatever was left, and make a home out of it, a home I could call my own, no matter where I go. ◆

BAKED CHICKEN ADOBO INFUSED WITH COCONUT MILK

This is a dish that was always ours. Long before Magellan's Spanish fleet set sail to the Spice Islands and fortuitously found the island of Cebu, the natives of the Philippines were already cooking adobo. The cooking method resembled one the Spanish recognized from home, so they called it adobo, derived from adobar, meaning "to marinate." And although it became known by its Spanish name, the dish itself is indigenously and distinctly Filipino. Adobo, like most Filipino dishes, is served with rice. This recipe offers a convenient variation: bread. Try serving it shredded on sliced bread topped with your favorite leafy greens.

PREPARATION TIME: 30 minutes + 1 hour to bake
YIELD: 4–6 servings

1 cup coconut milk

1 cup rice vinegar

¼ cup dark soy sauce

12 cloves garlic, chopped

1–2 chiles of your choice, seeded and diced

1 ½ teaspoons freshly ground black pepper

5 bay leaves

3–4 pounds bone-in, skin-on chicken thighs

8–12 slices bread, for serving

Combine the coconut milk, rice vinegar, soy sauce, garlic, chiles, black pepper, and bay leaves in a large Dutch oven. Add the chicken and turn to coat. Set aside at room temperature until the oven is heated.

Preheat the oven to 400°F.

Bake the adobo, uncovered, for about 1 hour, or until the meat is tender. Remove the adobo from the oven and discard the bay leaves.

Heat the broiler. Transfer the chicken pieces to a roasting pan or baking dish and broil for 5 to 7 minutes, until the skin is crisp and begins to caramelize. Flip the chicken, baste with the sauce from the pan, and broil for 3 to 5 minutes more.

Transfer the chicken to a platter and drizzle heavily with the remaining sauce. Serve immediately with the bread alongside, or shred the meat and make sandwiches.

Baked Chicken Adobo Infused with Coconut Milk (page 69)

Spaghetti Sauce Chicken Afritada (page 77)

MY AFRITADA ANGEL

THE TRIP TO my mother's homeland in the Philippines was my high school graduation gift. In the Philippines, Mom and I traveled from town to town to visit family, always with six or seven of my male cousins as my bodyguards. It may sound glamorous, but I assure you, it was not.

The state of poverty in some areas hit me hard straightaway. Big families crammed themselves into makeshift dwellings made of thin planks of wood and galvanized iron. Disabled people, women breastfeeding babies, and very young children in rags weaved through dangerous, traffic-laden roads, begging for money. Sadness and helplessness I had never felt before overpowered me; I couldn't bring myself to eat.

Three days. I didn't eat for three days. The only food I could manage to hold down was coconut water. Mom was so busy visiting people she hadn't seen in many years that she didn't notice I went without food. On the long journeys to remote towns, I fought back tears. I didn't want to look distraught when I met a new set of elders for the first time.

At one village with a row of small, fragile-looking thatched-roof huts, my mom left me to wander around outside with my bodyguards. The tang of food cooking filled the air. Nauseated, I headed to the outhouse around the corner, a good distance away from my bodyguards.

As I pushed the cardboard door to exit the bathroom, I heard a voice say, "I speak English." A woman, probably in her late 30s or early 40s, was standing under a palm tree, holding towels rolled up into a ball. I wondered how long she had been waiting for me to come out.

DALENA HASKINS
BENAVENTE was
born in Union City,
Tennessee, and
attended school in
the small town of Troy.
She received a BA
in communications
from the University of
Tennessee at Martin.
After moving to
California in her 20s,
she learned to cook,
which opened big
doors for her. She has
worked as a recipe de-
veloper and product
tester for Kraft, filmed
with Paula Deen, and
hosted numerous
cooking segments on
a variety of radio and
TV channels. Dalena's
first food memoir,
*Asian Girl in a South-
ern World*, recounts
her life growing up in
Tennessee as one of
the only Filipinos in
the area.

"You sick. You have fever. Too much coconut water. That's why you in the bathroom," she said with a chuckle. She spoke what I considered to be good English for a village native.

She approached me, unrolling a towel, which exposed a cold center as if it had originally held ice that had melted, and wiped my hands. She unrolled another towel and draped it around my neck. It was so cold it felt hot. She took my hand in hers, and we whizzed past my bodyguard cousins. With her eyebrows and lips, she ordered them with a "Pshhh!" and flicked her free hand in their direction, her way of saying, "Sit down. This is woman's business." It seemed as if she had abducted me. I looked back at my now-worthless bodyguards sitting on the ground, looking shamed to have been immobilized by this 98-pound woman who didn't even have to use a real word to do so.

Questions ran through my head. *Who is she? A village neighbor? A bossy cousin? A powerful madam who is going to sell me into prostitution? And where are we going?* I didn't know, but I went with her. I was confused, but I was too hot and sick to care.

She ushered me to a nearby hut and ducked her head to enter, pulling my hand behind her. I followed. She sat me in a clean wooden chair by the door, behind a long table cluttered with a few pots, a few bowls, and a bowl of three or four pristine tomatoes. She released my hand and walked to the other side of the table but remained standing. She picked up a spoon and lifted the lid of a small pot on the table. Steam billowed into the air. I understood. This small table was also her kitchen, and she had cooked food for me to eat. I opened my mouth to explain I wasn't hungry, but before I could speak, she said, "You have to eat. This is good. You feel better."

She scooped piping-hot, pillowy white rice into a bowl and topped it with chicken and potatoes in scarlet sauce. Clearly, she had invested time in planning this meal and getting me in there, but I didn't want it. The sickness was too strong. She moved next to me, holding the bowl carefully in both hands. She bowed her head, closed her eyes, prayed to Jesus in broken English, touched my forehead with her thumb, and said, "Amen."

She composed a bite onto the spoon and carefully blew on it, like a mother cooling down a bite for her baby. I looked down at it with dread. It was half a spoonful of brightly colored broth with flecks of black pepper. The steam beckoned to me like a wave of hello while I considered my doom. She held the spoon close and steady to my mouth, keeping her eyes focused on the spoon, careful not to spill a drop. After growing tired of holding her position, she crinkled her eyebrows and nodded her head sharply as if to say, "Open now!" much as she had ordered my cousins. Instantly, my mouth opened and the spoon was in and then out. I swallowed with my eyes shut tightly. I could feel her leaning toward my face to watch what would happen next. I exhaled out my nose, preparing for an aggravated nausea.

Then something happened. As I exhaled, the black pepper tingled my nose and traveled up to my brain, massaging my head with microscopic velvet bubbles. It stimulated my neck, eyes, and mind to relinquish my fever. The broth caressed my dry throat and esophagus with the flavors of warm tomato, sturdy bay leaf, and aromatic garlic, reawakening the path to my stomach with vitality. I relaxed my face but kept my eyes closed, appreciating the wonder of this one bite of food, aware that my body was coming back to life.

I opened my eyes. There she was, grinning with missing teeth. My eyes were more focused now and opened wider than they were before. She spoon-fed me one more bite, then handed me the bowl to feed myself. By the time I had eaten half, I felt like myself.

"Afritada," she said, now standing behind the table.

"What?"

"Afritada. You eat afritada. Remember it. Is very important. A-fri-tah-dah. Say it," she said.

"Afritada," I said. "Who are you?"

"I am a friend."

"Do you know my mom?"

"I know who she is."

"Are you family?"

"We're all family," she said. "Party tonight. That's what they talk about. They cooking for it. You have good time. No sick now. So dance! You dance tonight at party!" I didn't care about a party, but I agreed.

She smiled at me with love, like a proud mother looking at her child. Then she began cleaning and said, "Okay, you go," and flicked her hand up toward the door, signaling me to leave. It was awkward, but it didn't feel rude. I stood up. As I ducked my head to exit, I looked back at her. She was cleaning. Just cleaning, paying no attention to me.

I hurried over to where my cousins were sitting. They got to their feet as soon as they saw me coming.

"Who was that?"

"Who?" they asked.

"The woman," I said. They looked at each other.

"What woman?" one of them asked.

I was confused. Were they playing dumb?

"The woman who told you to sit down when I walked by."

There was silence. One of them scratched his head. They shifted their weight from side to side. "You told us to sit down," one said, "So we sit here, until you say. Smoke cigarette."

"You didn't see the woman?"

"No woman. Just you. Where you go?"

"With the woman!" They jumped back. I had never yelled at them before. "I'm so sorry," I said. "A woman was under the tree and took me over there." I pointed.

"Where?"

"Over there." I pointed again. "She fed me!" At this, they all seemed to panic.

I led them over to the shelter where I had just been. As we got closer, we could hear jovial voices and laughter coming from within. Pots and pans clunked.

Inside, seven or eight other women, one of them my mother, were preparing for something. My cousins began talking in Tagalog with another woman there, telling her my story about eating with someone alone in the very same place not too long ago. The lady glanced at me, then laughed out loud. "No!" she exclaimed, believing we were trying to play a trick on her. Mom came over to me.

"Oh. You're not sick now? We just decided to have a party tonight," she said. "We have to do a lot of cooking."

"Where's the fra-fri-tada?" I asked, trying to remember how the lady taught me to pronounce it.

"Afritada? We're going to make it now, but there's not a tomato in the entire village. We have to use spaghetti sauce."

I scanned the table where the fresh tomatoes had been just 10 or 15 minutes ago. Gone. In fact, nothing looked familiar except for the table that was now set up to butcher chicken. The chair I sat in was now in the corner, employed as a drying rack for wet towels.

"I had it already. Here," I said. "With the lady."

"No, we're going to cook it later. Don't worry. You go. Spend time with your cousins," she said, nudging me out the door. "Go buy ube ice cream for everyone."

I searched all afternoon and all night at the party for the lady. I never saw her. After obsessively asking people about her and not getting any answers, I didn't know what else to do. It was clear. No one cared. So, I did the only thing I knew to do, which was the only thing the mysterious lady instructed me to do other than eat. I danced. ◆

SPAGHETTI SAUCE CHICKEN AFRITADA

PREPARATION TIME: 1 hour
YIELD: 6–8 servings

Afritada, a traditional chicken and vegetable stew, is a gateway dish to Filipino cuisine. It's a great one to prepare when someone isn't familiar with traditional Filipino food because the core ingredients are classic flavors in almost every place in the world. It opens up the eater's mind to the possibility of what else Filipino food may have to offer. Spaghetti sauce, instead of fresh tomatoes or tomato sauce, is used in this recipe for convenience and taste.

¼ cup vegetable oil

6 cloves garlic, finely chopped

2 medium onions, halved and sliced into thin half-moons

4 pounds bone-in, skinless chicken pieces

3 large potatoes, peeled, halved lengthwise, and quartered crosswise

2 large carrots, coarsely chopped

2 cups unsalted chicken broth or water

1 (24-ounce) jar spaghetti sauce

½ cup soy sauce

2 teaspoons granulated sugar

1 teaspoon freshly ground black pepper

2 small bay leaves

2 red bell peppers, seeded and sliced into strips

1 green bell pepper, seeded and sliced into strips

2 tablespoons fish sauce, for serving (optional)

6–8 cups cooked white rice, for serving

In a large stockpot, heat the oil over medium-high heat. Add the garlic and onions and cook for 3 minutes, until the onions are soft.

Add the chicken pieces and cook for 3 to 5 minutes, turning occasionally, until the chicken is no longer raw on the outside.

Stir in the potatoes, carrots, chicken broth, spaghetti sauce, soy sauce, sugar, black pepper, and bay leaves. Stir well and bring the mixture to a boil. Reduce the heat to medium and cook, uncovered, for 20 minutes.

Add the bell peppers. Continue cooking for another 15 to 20 minutes, until the potatoes are fork tender.

Remove the afritada from the heat. Stir in the fish sauce, if using, and serve hot with the rice.

CHAPTER 3

MEAT

EONS BEFORE Fergus Henderson coined the phrase "nose to tail eating," Filipinos had already acquired the art of appreciating all parts of an animal by turning them into palatable dishes. The beast that ranks first and foremost in the Philippines' hierarchy of preference is the pig. Filipinos eat more pork than the global average—and almost five times more pork than beef. The nation's appetite for all things porcine existed way before the country was named the Philippines. Unlike cattle, which arrived in the country during the Spanish colonial period, pigs are indigenous to the land. In October 2008, Anthony Bourdain visited Cebu, Philippines, for his TV show *No Reservations*. Upon tasting the nation's iconic lechon, a whole hog skewered on a bamboo spit and slow roasted over charcoal, he declared it the "best pig ever."

THE MAKING OF LUMPIA

D AD, I HAVE something to tell you . . . I dropped out of engineering school.

I rehearse this line in my head, but it doesn't quite roll off the tongue. It's more like a slap in the face and a punch in the gut.

Telling any parent that you've dropped out of college to run a food truck is difficult enough. But if your parent is like my dad—an electrical engineer who grew up in the Philippines, a firm believer that success in life goes hand in hand with a degree—it's trouble. No wonder Filipinos are not known for entrepreneurship in the United States.

Sitting by myself on my bed, I'm a mess. Sweating, shaking, panicking, rethinking dropping out. Anxiety at an all-time high. *Maybe the school will take me back? Why did I think this was a good idea? Who drops out of engineering school to open a food truck? Maybe he won't be that pissed, just sort of pissed, but hopefully not try-to-break-a-chair-over-me pissed. Note to self: make sure he isn't chopping anything when you break the news.*

What would Dad do if he were in my shoes? His often-told beginnings with my mom come to mind: a story that took place way before I was born . . . way before I shatter my father's heart to bits . . . way before I'm stamped as the world's worst daughter.

It happened at Providence Hospital in Anchorage, Alaska. A nervous but interested Raymund, my father, thought Deb, one of the nurses, was attractive. The problem was, he was too shy to ask her out himself. So, he tried to find a way: butter up a coworker to do the job for him. Raymund bribed his colleague with the Filipino noodle dish called pansit, which quickly sealed the deal. Upon receiving Raymund's invite through the

ALEXA ALFARO
is an Alaska-born
Milwaukeean. In fifth
grade, Alexa took a
10-week trip to the
Philippines, which
opened her eyes and
inspired her to open
Meat on the Street,
Milwaukee's first
Filipino food truck, with
her brother Matthew
in 2014. After three
food truck seasons of
slinging BBQ sticks
and pork adobo, the
duo opened Meat on
the Street's brick-and-
mortar operation at
Eleven25, an old Pabst
Brewery building in
Milwaukee. The eldest
of three, Alexa grew
up in the kitchen
with her father. While
cooking has always
been her brother's
strength, Alexa can roll
lumpias and skewer
BBQs to her father's
expectations. Currently,
she half jokingly states,
"I skewer meat for a
living."

go-between, Deb, my independent, strong-willed, Italian-German Wisconsinite mother, laughed and said, "This isn't middle school."

Twenty-nine years of marriage and three children later, I'd say that what started with a middleman turned out, more or less, happily ever after, except for infuriating occasions when strangers asked Mom from where she had adopted her dark-haired, olive-skinned children—and possibly after I inform them I've quit school.

Taking inspiration from their story, I figure I'll test the water as Dad did with Mom. Mom, from whom I get my sass and strong-willed spirit, has always mediated between Dad and me. She'll be my perfect go-between.

I leave my room and find Mom in the living room. I tell her my plan. Her response? "Interesting." Well it isn't a WTF, are you on drugs, blah-blah, yell, yell. But it isn't words of encouragement or inspiration either. Thanks, Mom!

So much for mediation. Since that didn't work, I'm left with no choice but to grow a pair and speak with Dad.

There are three traits Dad and I bond over: our love for movies, our love for food, and our night-owl habits. Hence, since both of us are up until late in the night, we often hang out together making lumpia, a crunchy, savory, deep-fried Filipino-style egg roll stuffed with minced pork and vegetables. I prize eating lumpia just as much as I prize preparing it with Dad.

Here's a usual scene from our lumpia-making sessions: Dad juliennes carrots and chops cabbage with the flair of a pro, while I chop celery like a newbie. Dad's ease with the knife is remarkable; he can chop vegetables in uniform sizes with his eyes closed. With his thumb tucked behind his fingers, his curled fingertips grip the vegetable in place, guiding along the sharp instrument. Prepping always stirs up memories from his childhood.

"Lexa," he says, chopping away while he speaks and looks at me, "can you believe it? I grew up with one pair of shoes. One pair! For the entire year!"

This is a hard concept for me to grasp. I grew up with a shoe-aholic mother and, in turn, "Hi, I'm Alexa. I'm a shoe-aholic."

"You know my nanay, your lola, taught me everything I know," he says. "She taught all of us how to cook." My dad is one of 11. Raising all of them was no easy feat, so Lola ruled the house the best way she knew how—with an iron fist.

"Once . . . ," Dad warms up, setting a pan on the stove to heat. I know what story he's going to tell; I've heard it all my life but am eager to hear it once more. It's one of my favorites. "Your tito Ahl and I were tasked with cleaning the pigpen. In the pen was a boar—huge and mean. There was no way we could have carried out our chore unharmed. The boar would have killed us! Your lola, upon finding the pigpen uncleaned, was furious! She demanded to know why we didn't do as we were told."

Dad pauses as he tosses the ingredients for the lumpia filling into the pan, which steams and sizzles. No one dared cross Lola. Based on what I heard, Lola's punishments ranged from whacking the troublemaker with a broom to grabbing a guitar off the wall and slamming it over the head of the closest child, while the others ran for cover.

"'Nanay,' we pleaded, 'the boar won't let us. We tried, but it would charge at us if we as much as set foot in the pen.' Your lola would have none of this. She stopped what she was doing, went to the yard, and grabbed a two-by-four."

At this point of his story, Dad bursts into laughter and can barely get the part out about how Lola marched into the pen, two-by-four in hand, and the boar charged at her. Without hesitation, she showed the hog who the boss was by walloping it with the plank. The story always ends like this: "That boar never gave us any trouble after that. When Lola walked toward the pen, it squealed with fear."

Making lumpia is a process. Storytelling accompanies every part of it, from prepping and cooking to wrapper peeling, rolling, and deep-frying. With every step of the process, I learn more about Dad, my roots, and our food. He often speaks about cooking with his nanay. Of family parties that lasted for days. Of long buffet tables of food. I, in turn, open up about my day, school, friends, and so on. We chat away, but keep working. It feels as if I could talk to Dad about anything. . . .

Right, it's time for me to face my boar. I can do this. It'll be okay. What's the worst that could happen? No. Let's not go there now. Okay, now Mom is present: good. But he is chopping: not good. I'll sit across from him. A breakfast bar in between should be enough of a safe distance.

Mom sits next to me and shoots me a nervous glance. My dad is making dinner. This is his therapy. After a day's work, he loves to come home and cook.

My heart pounds against my chest. I swear he can hear it.

"Lexa!" my dad says in a loud tone with authority.

This is it. I'm a goner.

"Have you seen the latest episode of *Survivor*?" he asks.

Whew! Well, I have at least a couple more minutes.

I mutter something incomprehensible. I'm stalling as best as I can. My palms are sweating, hands shaking, and heart's still pounding. I try to swallow before breaking the news. There is a lump so big, I feel I may choke. Sounds better than doing what I'm about to do. Mom nudges me hard as soon as my dad opens the fridge. He's jolly and happy, rambling on about something irrelevant to the panic raging inside me. Mom gives me that you-must-tell-him-now look.

"Dad, I need to tell you something."

He's back at the stove, stirring something in a pot. It smells good at least. Hopefully he will let me eat dinner before he throws me out of the house.

He turns around. "Okay . . . ?" He looks from me to Mom.

"Don't look at me," says my mom. "This wasn't my idea." *Thanks, Mom, once again.*

"I decided to postpone finishing my degree." He stares at me blankly. *Say something, please. At least another "Okay . . . ," maybe followed up by a "Why?"*

"I've been doing some thinking, soul searching, and engineering isn't going to make me long-term happy."

"Okay, then, what is?" Still waiting for the bomb to drop. Damn my parents for knowing me so well.

"Well, my longest job was at a steak house, and I've always loved the food and beverage industry. I did my research. There is no Filipino food in Milwaukee. None. Nothing even close; Madison and Chicago are the closest. And a food truck would be a great way to test the market. It is fairly inexpensive to start, compared to a restaurant. Less risk. I was thinking Matthew and I could run it, see what happens, create a concept around all the favorite dishes we grew up eating.

"I've even bought an LLC, see? I'm very serious about this. I have documents on how to do everything, building the truck, paperwork, branding, social media presence. . . ."

About three months later, we make our way to the northwest side of Milwaukee. Snow is falling. A solid four to five inches already covers the ground. I, with the help of Dad, buy a former We Energies truck from a man who changed his mind about opening a bakery food truck.

It's how a Filipino food truck in Wisconsin was born. And how memories are shared and created, family ties are secured and strengthened, and dreams become reality through the making of lumpia. ◆

LUMPIA

PORK AND VEGETABLE EGG ROLLS

PREPARATION TIME: 1½ hours + 30 minutes to cool
YIELD: 50–75 egg rolls

2 tablespoons canola oil, plus more for deep-frying

2 medium sweet onions, thinly sliced

6 cloves garlic, minced

1 pound ground pork

1 bunch celery, trimmed and thinly sliced

8 carrots, cut into thin strips

1½ teaspoons freshly ground black pepper

¼ cup fish sauce

2 heads (about 5 pounds) green cabbage, thinly sliced

1 (28-ounce) package frozen French-cut green beans, thawed

50–75 square egg roll wrappers

Sweet chile sauce, for serving (optional)

No Filipino gathering is complete without them. Lumpia is a catchall name for food rolled in an egg roll wrapper. There are as many kinds of lumpia in the Philippines as there are kinds of fillings. A few of them are not fried, such as lumpiang sariwa, or fresh lumpia, in which the egg roll is filled with stir-fried vegetables, and lumpiang ubod, or lumpia stuffed with hearts of palm. Fried lumpias include lumpiang saging, aka turon, a sweet banana lumpia, and lumpiang shanghai, aka lumpia, the Filipino version of the egg roll. Traditionally, the uncooked filling of lumpiang shanghai is bound together by an egg, wrapped, and then deep-fried. This recipe, however, calls for the filling to be stir-fried before it's rolled and deep-fried. The extra step eliminates the risk of ending up with a raw-cored egg roll.

In a large wok or sauté pan with high sides, heat the oil over medium heat until it shimmers. Add the onions and cook for about 2 minutes, or until they are semitranslucent. Stir in the garlic and cook for about 2 minutes, or until it is light gold.

Add the ground pork. Cook, stirring and breaking up the clumps, until the pork turns from pink to brown. Add the celery, carrots, pepper, and fish sauce. Mix for 2 minutes. Stir in the cabbage and green beans and cook, stirring continuously, for about 5 minutes, or until the cabbage is starting to soften but still slightly crunchy.

Mix the filling thoroughly one last time. Pour the mixture into a strainer set over the sink and let drain and cool for about 30 minutes, stirring occasionally, until no longer warm to the touch.

Meanwhile, peel apart all the wrappers. Place them under a damp cloth to keep them moist while you work.

Recipe continues >

Lay one wrapper on your work surface so that it looks like a diamond. Place a heaping tablespoon of the filling across the wrapper, about an inch from the bottom corner and a half inch from both side corners. Fold the bottom corner up over the filling and roll once. Tuck both sides in and then roll all the way up tightly. Moisten the top corner of the wrapper with water to seal. Repeat with the remaining filling and egg roll wrappers. The egg rolls can be deep-fried immediately or stored in the freezer for a month or more for future use. Pack them without overlapping in freezer containers or zip-top bags.

In a large, deep saucepan, pour in about 3 inches of canola oil, or enough to completely submerge the egg rolls. Heat the oil over medium-high heat until a deep-fry thermometer registers 350°F. Working in batches, add a few of the egg rolls in a single layer and deep-fry until they are golden brown, about 5 minutes. Use a slotted spoon or tongs to transfer them to paper towels to drain. Repeat this process with the remaining egg rolls. Serve warm with the sweet chile sauce, if using.

POUNDING ON THE DOOR WITH
A SLEDGEHAMMER

ORDER SLIPS STACK UP in the window of the pirate ship that is our cramped, rectangular restaurant kitchen. Music by Odd Future, Doom, and Pusha T blares from the subwoofer. A crew of Ecuadorian dishwashers run up the stairs with sauté pans, and the bearded Arkansans I cook for shout: "Fire a shorty, let me know when it's five minutes out. Carlos, más platos! Braulio, what the fuck is going on? Why are they only selling one item? Tell them to sell other shit."

It is a busy Saturday night in the Lakeview neighborhood on Chicago's North Side, and I am finally cooking Filipino food professionally. Nursing fresh cuts on my fingers and burns on my forearms is no excuse for slacking. Whatever it takes to get that beef short rib adobo in the window piping hot and looking pretty is what you do.

After suffering that ass-kicking in the kitchen, I stand in the snow, a frigid February wind blistering my face, smoking a Bugler with a punk rock band roadie turned server. You'd think we were Catholics from the Dark Ages with penchants for masochism as we put ourselves through a sort of odd penance while cooking. As the train nears and I throw my hand-rolled cigarette into a snow bank, the only thing on my mind, aside from the bar I am headed to, are my memories of food, when it all started, and the experiences that shaped my craft.

I grew up in California in the late '80s in the Filipino community of Stockton and Lathrop. At that time in South Stockton, growing up in a Filipino family meant you were barely one generation removed from Jim Crow, and your family worked in the fields, the canneries, or the seasonal jobs available in Alaska. Oh yeah, and did I mention that your parties

ROBERT MENOR was born in 1984 at Malmstrom Air Force Base in Great Falls, Montana. He is a mestizo (mixed blood) of Filipino and Mexican heritage. Raised in South Stockton, California, and currently residing in Columbus, Ohio, with his family, he spent 12 years in Chicago in and out of hospitality jobs before deciding to cook seriously. He attended the Cooking and Hospitality Institute of Chicago and is now the head chef at Bonifacio, a modern Filipino restaurant in Columbus, Ohio. Robert is also the founder of the ATANG Filipino food pop-up and catering company, and he spearheads the Little Manila Culinary Council.

were huge and prep often began a day before? My favorite prep was the parti kalding, or goat butchering. Slightly after dawn you'd hear a flame-thrower and men shouting in Ilocano, the largest Filipino spoken dialect next to Visayan in Stockton. This was the alarm clock of everything. This not only woke me up for the day, but it woke up the part of me that would become a cook dedicated to Filipino food and preservation of the culture.

Before each big gathering, my grandma Sabina made an atang, a food offering to ancestors, family, or those who came and left before us. It consisted of whatever food we prepared that day, along with rice, a boiled egg, and a drink. The atang connected everything for me as far as food, spirituality, and our culture were concerned. Oftentimes, she prepared large pots of pinakbet, a mixed vegetable stew, and aba (also known as laing), taro leaves stewed in coconut milk, and baked a lot of hopia, sweet pastries similar to Chinese mooncakes, made with red mung beans or a delicacy known as coconut sport. Most of our food was grown in the garden: taro, banana leaves, eggplant, bitter melon, kabocha squash, lemons, and pomelos.

When Grandma made adobo, it was always a special treat because she rarely prepared meat dishes. This was probably how I came to think of adobo as a highly coveted meal even though it was a common dish. Sometimes, my grandma's sister, who raised chickens for food, butchered them fresh to make adobo. The aroma of meat stewing and developing flavor in vinegar and soy sauce made it even more sought after. Filipino cooking passed along from family member to family member, so this had been my culinary school before I went to culinary school.

Almost 20 years later, here I am in Chicago, firing up one adobo order after another in a pirate ship restaurant. My mustache is larger, my list of problems is longer, my attitude is tougher, and the chips are stacked high on my shoulder. I'm an adult in a new city with my hometown on my back as I go at it with the rest of the world. I am happy to finally be in a similar setting to where I came from, as far as diversity and flavors go.

Being a line cook under the tutelage of some of the finest chefs has started to rub off on me. When I'm not jazz club–hopping or getting kicked out of places only a hipster can love, I'm fine-tuning my memories into recipes while incorporating techniques learned on the line.

Always keeping my ear to the street, I hear about a contest called Adobofest in Chicago. The winner from the previous year is a coworker of mine, and I feel that it is time for me to add some more credentials to my name. The result is a marriage of Filipino technique and Southwestern US styles that I call adobo loko. This creation ends up making its debut at the 2013 Adobofest and fares well with the younger, more progressive crowds.

This experience teaches me what works for whom, and where to focus my efforts. It also teaches me to tune out certain crowds, those who are bound by prejudgments and crab mentalities; I deem them useless in the advancement of our food and culture based on their comments: "Oh, he's Mexican, so he's cooking the Mexican way, not the real Filipino way."

I realize it's time for me to take a proactive role—to continue cooking and educating open-minded people about our culture through food. Everything, from how I host a pop-up dinner to the explanations behind every dish I create, helps me change things that I think are wrong in our culture—where, sadly, habits are bent on resenting others' accomplishments and pulling each other down. The adobo loko serves as an introduction. It is an example of how I go deeper into a world as a Fil-American chef by pounding on the door with a sledgehammer of pulled pork adobo. ◆

PULLED PORK ADOBO LOKO SLIDERS

PREPARATION TIME: 10 minutes + 7 hours to braise and rest

YIELD: 6–8 servings

Here's a pulled pork version of adobo with similarities to lechon paksiw, a sweet-and-sour stew made from leftover roast pig, and humba, a sweet meat stew. I recommend garnishing this dish with a green papaya and carrot pickle known as atchara, which needs to be started at least five days ahead of time. Try pairing the meal with ginger tea or a pilsner.

1 (4-pound) pork cushion (also called picnic shoulder)

6 tablespoons brown sugar

2½ tablespoons paprika

4 star anise

3 bay leaves

1 head garlic, crushed

1 tablespoon whole cloves

1 tablespoon whole black peppercorns

1 cup soy sauce

¾ cup spiced vinegar (see Note on page 93)

⅓ cup water

12–16 slider buns

Atchara (recipe follows), for serving (optional)

Preheat the oven to 300°F.

Rub the pork all over with the brown sugar and paprika. Heat a large skillet over high heat. Add the pork and sear each side for about 2 minutes, or until reddish brown. Watch this closely, as the sugar may burn if you aren't attentive. Transfer the pork to a roasting pan.

Wrap the anise, bay leaves, garlic, cloves, and peppercorns in a sachet made of cheesecloth and add it to the pan. Then add the soy sauce, vinegar, and water.

Seal the roasting pan with plastic wrap and then aluminum foil and braise for 6 hours. Transfer the adobo to a platter and set it aside to rest for 1 hour. Reserve the sauce and discard the sachet of seasonings.

Shred the meat, place it on a plate, and cover it with the reserved warmed sauce.

Fill the buns with the adobo. Garnish with atchara, if using, and serve.

Pulled Pork Adobo Loko Sliders (page 91)

ATCHARA

2 tablespoons rock salt

1 pound green papaya, peeled, seeded, and grated

2 cups granulated sugar

4 cups white vinegar

1 large carrot, peeled and grated

1 green bell pepper, seeded and thinly sliced

2 cloves garlic

1 (2-inch) piece ginger, peeled and sliced

Mix the salt and papaya in a bowl and set it aside for about 1 hour.

Combine the sugar and vinegar in a 3-quart saucepan. Bring to a boil over medium heat, stir, and boil until the sugar is completely dissolved. Remove from the heat and set aside to cool to room temperature.

Transfer the salted papaya to a strainer and rinse under running water. Drain the papaya well and transfer to a piece of cheesecloth. Wrap the cheesecloth around the papaya and squeeze out as much liquid as possible.

Mix the papaya with the carrot, bell pepper, garlic, and ginger in a large bowl. Transfer the papaya mixture to sterilized jars (see Notes). Pour the reserved sugar and vinegar mixture over the papaya until it is completely submerged in liquid.

Seal the jars and refrigerate for at least 5 days before using. The atchara will keep in the refrigerator for months.

NOTES: Spiced vinegar is white vinegar infused with chiles, onion, and garlic and can be found at Asian grocery stores.

Sterilizing jars is easy. Simply wash the jars and without drying them, pop them in a 320°F oven for 15 minutes.

Toasted Filipino bread rolls called *pandesal* or *pan de sal*, which literally means "bread of salt," are a great alternative to slider buns. Packaged ready-made pandesal are available in most Asian-Filipino stores.

THE MIGHTY CLUB OF MIGHTOR

{AS TOLD TO THE EDITOR}

I WILL NEVER make it on time, I thought. Blood deluged my left hand's food prep glove—again.

I had just finished trimming a pork leg using my brand-new, state-of-the-art, sponsored set of Japanese Tamahagane knives. Without applying much pressure, the knives sliced, chopped, and peeled like a dream, until one of the harakiri-sharp blades ripped through the flesh of my forefinger. Since then, it had gotten leaky pretty quickly.

Representing Norway at one of the five sleek cooking stations equipped with the latest kitchen appliances, I battled against four other chefs from Denmark, Sweden, Finland, and Iceland for the title of Nordic Chef of the Year. With every tick of the clock, my adrenaline pumped harder and blood squirted out faster from my slit capillaries. A medic rushed to my aid for the second time. My wound required re-treating, re-dressing, and regloving every hour, eating up a big chunk of my time in the five- to six-hour competition.

I had trained painstakingly for this event. I had rehearsed each step, timed each task, and mastered each technique meticulously. Two hours into the cook-off, however, and I still had big tasks ahead of me. It would take a superhuman effort to pull this off.

Wounded, I soldiered on to make up for lost time. I'd be lying, though, if I said that my handicap didn't bother me. Nothing could replace direct hands-on contact in establishing a connection with my ingredients. I was used to cutting and working by feel. I needed to run my fingers along the surface of the meat, feel the grain and the tightness of the muscle, and massage salt and spices onto the skin and

Chef CHRISTIAN ANDRE PETTERSEN is the son of a Norwegian father and a Filipino mother. His identity, persona, and profession stem from his origins: a seamless fusion of East and West. Christian started his training in the kitchen at a very young age at his father's restaurant. His father, a chef, has been his idol and inspiration all throughout his career. By the time Christian turned 26, he had won 11 gold medals, eight silvers, and one bronze in prestigious regional, national, and continental culinary competitions, including S. Pellegrino Young Chef and Bocuse d'Or Norge 2017. In 2017 he was also honored as one of *Forbes* magazine's "30 under 30 Europe." He is currently the head chef at Mondo restaurant in Sandnes, Norway.

the flesh with my fingers. The gauze and glove that wrapped my hand stood in the way.

The inspiration for my main course was crispy pata, or pork leg, my mother's ancestral dish. I was maybe six when Mother took me to the Philippines for the first time, and next to the lechon (a whole roasted suckling pig), this was the dish I remembered most vividly.

Our relatives organized a lavish feast to celebrate our arrival. They had apparently prepared for this occasion for days. The dizzying variety and quantity of food laid out on a long table was in stark contrast to the modest conditions of the venue. I had no idea we had such a huge family and had never seen so many folks in one gathering. There were probably more people in that village shack than in the entire town of Bodø, the place in the northern part of Norway where I was born and raised. Most of all, I was overwhelmed by the warm, almost celebrity-like welcome we received from people whom I had never met before.

The centerpiece of the smorgasbord was a lechon—complete with eyes, ears, snout, and a bright red apple stuck in its mouth. The animal looked exactly as its living self, except for the honey-colored toasted skin. Poor thing! I couldn't bring myself to eat it. Next to the lechon, though, was a child-friendlier dish: golden-brown club-shaped meat on the bone, which reminded me of the cartoon caveboy Tor. When he held his club aloft and called out the name "Mightor," he was transformed into kick-ass superhero Mighty Mightor.

I picked up a club by its bone, bit into it like a caveboy, and heard a crackle when my teeth broke through the crust. The meat, in contrast to the skin, was tender and succulent. It was delightful.

"Only two hours to go!" announced the speaker, further energizing the already pumped cheftestants and audience. My heart pounded at super-G speed. The heat intensified in the kitchen. My chef's whites clung to my body, and my toque-imprisoned hair misted with sweat. It felt as if we were in the tropical Philippines rather than arctic Denmark. The concoction of scents swirling around the hall reminded me of a traditional Norwegian Christmas: pork roasting, cinnamon, cloves, nutmeg, and ginger.

To my dismay, the meat I rolled in its knuckle skin was not as tightly wrapped as I wanted it to be. And there was no time to redo it. For a moment, all I could think of were the people I would be letting down: the entourage who flew from Norway to Denmark to support me; acclaimed celebrity chef Eyvind Hellstrøm, who came to see me train in Stavanger; sponsors who put their trust in me; and, most especially, my father, a former chef and restaurant owner with whom I had made a pact.

My career in the kitchen had started at the age of nine. While my friends ran laps from goal box to goal box on a soccer pitch, I ran back and forth between the dishwashing and preparation stations of my father's restaurant kitchen. While they switched roles between forward, midfielder, and defender, I alternated between scraping plates, loading them in the dishwasher, scouring pots and pans, peeling sacks of potatoes and onions, scaling fish, and debearding mussels. Year after year, my passion for cooking soared along with my duties in Father's kitchen.

Ironically, as I drew closer to the age when I should be thinking about what studies to pursue, Father urged me to take up law or chiropractic medicine. His 50 arduous years working as a chef and restaurateur boiled down to bankruptcy, and he didn't want me to go down the same path. I was, however, already deeply entrenched in my culinary dream and couldn't shake it out of my system. After a long discussion, I convinced Father I had what it took to succeed in this cutthroat occupation. I promised him I would become the best of the best.

At 16, I attended culinary school, and by the time I reached 17, I was offered an apprenticeship at the restaurant of Bocuse d'Or champ Charles Tjessem. This meant moving to the west coast, a two-hour flight

My career in the kitchen had started at the age of nine. While my friends ran laps from goal box to goal box on a soccer pitch, I ran back and forth between the dishwashing and preparation stations of my father's restaurant kitchen.

from home. Though in financial difficulty, Father scraped up every cent he could gather to pay for plane tickets, for a decent apartment close to my place of work, for furniture, and for a month's worth of food and supplies. Lugging my belongings, Father accompanied me to my new location. He stayed with me for three days and did everything in his power to cushion my transition to independence, chefdom, and manhood.

When the time came for him to leave, he walked up to me and wrapped his arms around me. In that brief hug, I could sense his heart breaking. Giving me a pat on the back, he could muster no more than the words "Goodbye, son. Take care" in a brittle, low voice. I heard him sniff as he swiftly turned away and picked up his bag. He was gone. The cord was cut, but it felt as if the pair of scissors that severed the link was still stuck in my stomach.

"Only one hour to go!"

The crowd broke into cheers, whistles, and applause. Announcements blasted from the speakers, and judges rose to their feet, intruding station after station: they peeked into the ovens, peered into the fridges, lifted lids from pots, and inspected everything. I, on the other hand, tuned out. My mantra, "winners never quit, quitters never win," echoed in my head. In a bubble, I juggled multiple tasks on the double, like a chef on steroids. I kept an eye on the pig's skin crackling in the skillet and the meat braising in the oven while I shredded kohlrabi into strands to resemble Filipino pansit noodles. And there was also a starter and dessert to whip up—a gazillion more tasks to do and only a few minutes left.

"Third place goes to . . . Sweden!"

"Second place goes to . . . Denmark!"

The chef awardees, with medals on their chests, stood on the right and left podiums. Only one podium was left unmanned. A sinking sensation engulfed me. *I blew my chance.*

"And now, ladies and gentlemen, the Nordic Chef of the Year is . . . Christian Andre Pettersen of Norway!"

Cries of joy, thunderous clapping, and an explosion of confetti ensued. Clutching a trophy, plaque, and an oversize check, I took my place on the center podium and let out a victory roar.

Crispy pata, the inspiration for one of my dishes, had brought me the gold. The dish, on second thought, meant more to me than that. It was not about winning. It was about giving. My folks in the Philippines, and my father especially, had given so much when they had so little. Like them, I could—because often, we've got more in us than we think—draw from an unlimited source of strength. They and the people who invested their time, money, and effort in me are my source of power. Just like Tor's club, I hold them aloft, call upon them in my head, and magically, the Mighty Mightor in me gets unleashed. ◆

< Christian's original masterpiece, a take on crispy pata.

CRISPY PATA

BRAISED BONELESS PORK HOCKS WITH CRISPY PORK
RIND, GINGER–SOY GLAZE, AND TURNIP–APPLE SLAW

*Chef Christian's recipe,
inspired by crispy
pata, had 11 compo-
nents—oven-braised
boneless pork hocks,
onion compote, pork
crackling, a soy glaze, a
pork demi-glace, truffle
potato cream and mush-
rooms, cabbage-truffle
foie gras, artichoke
chips, turnip-apple
slaw, carrot quinoa, and
lingonberry powder—all
pieced together from
scratch. The resulting
dish is a masterpiece,
but it also requires the
skills of a master chef.
This simplified version,
adapted from Chris-
tian's recipe, is more
home-cook friendly. Ask
your butcher to bone the
pork hocks for you to
make it even simpler.*

PREPARATION TIME: 1 hour + 3 hours to braise and roast

YIELD: 4 servings

PORK HOCKS

2 (2½-pound) pork hocks, trimmed of excess fat and boned

Fine sea salt, to taste

2 tablespoons vegetable oil, divided, plus more for brushing

1 carrot, chopped

2 onions, chopped

2 celery ribs, chopped

2 cups chicken broth

2 cups beef broth

1 sprig thyme

10 whole black peppercorns

6 star anise

TURNIP-APPLE SLAW

2 teaspoons granulated sugar

2 apples, peeled, cored, and chopped

4 teaspoons salted butter

Juice of 1 lemon (about 3 tablespoons), divided

1 teaspoon apple cider vinegar

1 tablespoon olive oil

1 teaspoon prepared horseradish

Fine sea salt, to taste

4 small turnips, peeled and shredded

1 bunch cilantro, stemmed, for garnish

GINGER-SOY GLAZE

1 tablespoon vegetable oil

1 (2-inch) piece ginger, peeled and grated

2 tablespoons dark soy sauce

2 tablespoons honey

2 tablespoons balsamic vinegar

1 teaspoon freshly ground black pepper, plus more to taste

½ teaspoon cornstarch mixed with 1 teaspoon cold water

GARNISH

Crumbled chicharron (pork rind)

Recipe continues >

Make the pork hocks: Preheat the oven to 300°F.

Season the pork hocks all over with salt.

Heat 1 tablespoon of the oil in a Dutch oven over medium-high heat. Add the hocks and sear all over. Remove the hocks and set aside.

Pour the remaining 1 tablespoon of oil in the Dutch oven. Add the carrot, onions, and celery and cook, stirring, until slightly caramelized, about 20 minutes. Add the chicken and beef broths, thyme, peppercorns, and star anise. Stir and scrape any brown bits stuck to the bottom of the pot.

Return the hocks to the Dutch oven. Bring the mixture to a simmer, then cover and transfer to the oven. Braise for 2 hours 45 minutes, or until the meat is fork tender.

While the pork hocks braise, make the turnip-apple slaw: In a nonstick saucepan, heat the sugar, without stirring, over medium heat until it melts. Add the apples and stir until evenly coated with the molten sugar. Add the butter, 1½ teaspoons of the lemon juice, and the apple cider vinegar. Cook until all the liquid has evaporated, about 10 minutes. Remove the pan from the heat and let cool.

Whisk together the olive oil, the remaining 2½ tablespoons of lemon juice, and the horseradish in a bowl. Taste and add salt as needed. Before serving, toss the turnips and cooled apples in this dressing and garnish with the cilantro.

When the hocks are done, remove the pot from the oven.

Move an oven rack to the top position in the oven. Turn the broiler on high.

Remove the hocks from the broth and set aside to cool. Carefully peel off the skin without breaking it into pieces. Scrape off the fat and discard. Pat the skin dry, then prick all over with a knife or fork. Rub and press salt into the skin, making sure it penetrates the holes. Set the skin aside.

Strain and reserve ½ cup of the braising broth for the glaze and discard the rest.

Pull the meat from the bones and transfer the meat to an 8½ × 4½-inch loaf pan. Fill the pan only about an inch high. Press down on the meat with the base of a glass to form a compact block. Cut the meat into four equal portions.

Cut four pieces of the pork skin to the proper size to fit on top of each portion of meat in the loaf pan. Top the meat with the skin and brush the skin with oil. Secure the ends of the pieces of skin with toothpicks to prevent them from curling. Broil for 15 to 20 minutes, until the skin crackles and crisps. Remove from the oven.

Make the glaze: Heat the oil in a small saucepan over medium-high heat until it shimmers. Add the ginger and stir-fry until fragrant, about 30 seconds. Add the reserved ½ cup braising broth, soy sauce, honey, vinegar, and black pepper. Stir and bring to a simmer. Reduce the heat to low and add the cornstarch slurry. Continue stirring and simmering, tasting and adjusting the seasoning as needed, for about 5 minutes, or until the glaze is slightly thickened. Remove from the heat and strain.

Serve each portion of the pork topped with the glaze. Sprinkle with crumbled pork rind and accompany with the turnip-apple slaw.

IN LOVE AND REVOLUTION

I AM A MARTIAL-LAW BABY, born in the Philippines in 1973. My siblings and I are considered children of the storm, in reference to the First Quarter Storm, when the Ferdinand Marcos regime used civil unrest to justify a military takeover and suspension of ordinary law. Martial law was lifted in 1981, but it took the People Power Revolution of 1986 to topple the Marcos government. We moved to the United States that same year.

Prior to immigrating, we lived in Manila and, like most middle-class families, we celebrated birthdays and graduations by eating out. Kamayan, named after a Tagalog word meaning "eating with one's hands," had always been our go-to restaurant for specialty Filipino foods like kare-kare, a rich oxtail stew. In my earliest memories of Kamayan, I needed a step stool to wash my hands in basins made of giant taklobo clamshells. I remember inhaling the scent of steaming-hot rice on banana leaves set before us at a communal table, and our mother ladling kare-kare stew the color of a tropical sunset out of round clay pots. Each mouthful of tender oxtail meat, crunchy bok choy, and butter-soft eggplant, all coated in that velveteen peanut sauce tinted with red annatto seeds and made savory by fried shrimp paste, was reason enough to feel festive.

It seemed as though the entire nation were in a mood to celebrate in the last days of the dictatorship. People from all walks of life joined together for a common cause: from janitorial workers and university students to aging matrons from gated communities. My father was out on the streets as an investigative journalist for the Asian Social Institute,

VANESSA DEZA
HANGAD is a California-
based Filipina American
writer who spent five
years of living the good
expat life in Singapore.
Prior to focusing on
creative pursuits, she
worked for software and
health care companies.
Her poetry and prose
have been published
in *The Very Inside*, the
2017 Popular Readers'
Choice–nominated
*Singapore Love
Stories, Tales of Two
Cities: Singapore and
Hong Kong*, and UC
Berkeley's *{m}aganda*
magazine. She was also
a contributing writer
for *Asian Books Blog*
and has published
flash fiction in *Literary
Kitchen*. Vanessa is
working with a literary
agent as she completes
her first novel, *Alapaap*,
a family saga set in
the Philippines and the
United States.

coming home flushed with excitement at the triumph of People Power. We listened to "Onward Christian Soldiers" on Radio Veritas and waited for the unfolding drama in the newspapers. My favorite front-page article contained an image of a nun in full habit, clasping her rosary and inserting flowers into the barrel of an Armalite. The gun-toting soldier looked as though he were about to cry. I was 12 years old, and my kuya, or older brother, was 14. Our other siblings, a six-year-old brother and a sister who had just turned two, were too young to understand what was going on. But for Kuya and me, politics found its way into playtime. Kuya pretended to be pro-Marcos, flashing the V sign for victory. I wore yellow and countered with L, which stood for Laban, or Fight. As the excitement over a regime change took over the country, even my younger siblings joined me and Kuya (who was never a true Marcos loyalist anyway) in memorizing new political slogans like "Tama na! Sobra na! Palitan na!" ("Enough! Too Much! Replace already!") In solidarity with Cory Aquino, who would later ascend to the highest office of the land, our mother led her brood to tie yellow ribbons around Meralco electric posts for lack of old oak trees growing in our suburb of Quezon City.

Shortly after the fall of Marcos, we celebrated my 13th birthday with kare-kare at Kamayan. I gave a tearful speech at my elementary school graduation, because it was not only the end of a chapter but also the beginning of something completely unknown. In late June, we packed our belongings and immigrated to the United States, spending the summer with relatives who lived in California. By August, we were saying goodbye again, this time to Disneyland and sunset walks along Torrance Beach, and hello to our new life in Wichita, Kansas. My grandparents on my dad's side, who petitioned for us to immigrate to America, were in nearby Tulsa, Oklahoma. Kare-kare was the first celebratory food my mother made for us in the yellow starter home that we rented from her sister. Our bodies, born and bred in the tropics, needed the warmth of a hearty meal along with the hand-me-down jackets from our cousins. It was autumn, the first unfamiliar season we were to experience. Everything felt a little strange. There were grumpy squirrels in the oak tree in our front yard, jackrabbits that dashed away to the Baptist church next door, and casual racism at Robinson Junior High. I was interrogated in the hallways with "You're not white. You're not black. What are you?" I thought about the nun facing down her opponents, roses disarming weapons.

At first, I was too busy trying to fit in at my new school to notice how my mom cooked our food in Kansas. In the Philippines, we grew up with maids and extended family members. Food prep was never a chore we had to worry about. One thing I'd had to learn in America was how to help out in the kitchen—first, out of necessity, and then eventually, out of love for cooking. I now have the kare-kare recipe that my mother has perfected over the years, but I wanted to know how she made it that first year away from the Philippines. She has sparse recollections at best, so I emailed my father to find out what he remembers about our immigration story and, more importantly, his take on Mom's kare-kare in Kansas. He said, "We moved to the States after the great, glorious Philippine revolution of 1986. The Philippines was now supposedly freed from the shackles of a dictatorship. Or so we thought. . . . There were Oriental stores . . . where your mom most likely got her ingredients. The secret to good kare-kare is the ground peanuts. Maybe a little peanut butter also helps. The tripe must be well cooked, together with pig tail and knuckles. To get a thicker sauce, you can also use cow tail and pata," or pig's feet.

Spoken out loud, my family name, Deza, and the acronym for the People Power Revolution, EDSA, are anagrams. In the mid-'80s, a new dawn had also come for my family. My grandparents' petition was granted; after many years of waiting, we were to join them in America as immigrants. And so we uprooted instead of putting our stakes in the ground of a newly democratized Philippines. Opportunities in the United States were a stronger pull than the blueprint promised by the sainted woman at the helm of the republic. In the beginning, my parents chose the practical over theoretical, but in nations, as in families, conflicting ideologies can erode the ideal.

When we first moved to the United States, my parents had envisioned building a life together. But like the disappointment my father expressed in the aftermath of the 1986 revolution, what starts out as joyous can sometimes sour, especially when certain issues are swept aside. Dad was a University of the Philippines Diliman graduate, an activist who never quite shook off his university idealism, while Mom, who introduced him to left-leaning politics in their youth, became a pragmatist when she had children. My father had trouble finding his niche in America. After six years of going back and forth to the Philippines, where he answered the call to nation building as a writer and educator, then coming back to family life and unfulfilling work in Los Angeles, where we finally settled down, he moved back to the Philippines for good.

My mother has thrived in United States. She had a successful career as a health care administrator and business owner before she switched her focus to helping with the care of her grandchildren. She is a survivor and an inspiration, the matriarch known for the wonders she concocts in her kitchen. She is a force to be reckoned with when shopping for fresh vegetables at the Torrance Farmers' Market and finding the best cuts of meat at 99 Ranch Market in Gardena. She uses only oxtail and considers pork hocks and feet less desirable ingredients. She gilds the lily sometimes by topping the finished kare-kare with good French butter. In the land of plenty, kare-kare becomes an exercise in glorious excess. Like every child of an accomplished cook, I prefer my mother's version. I consider Mom's kare-kare superior to even my best memories of the same dish from our favorite restaurant.

Sometimes I wonder what would have become of us had we stayed in the Philippines. How many more celebratory meals of kare-kare would we have had at Kamayan? Would we have remained the unassailable nuclear family I had so idealized? When my father left California for good, I was already a sophomore at UC Berkeley and preoccupied with life as an undergrad. I didn't feel the pain of his absence in the same way as other members of my family. But his choice to leave has also left its mark on me. I've processed the disappointment and have turned my heartbreak into an opportunity to confront and eventually reconnect. After many years of living and working in the United States, I've returned to the region of my birth as a Filipina American expat in Singapore with my husband and our young son. Now that my father is less than three hours away in Manila, he's joined us for vacations in Bali and has stayed with us in Singapore. I see my mother and siblings once a year during the holidays when we fly back to California. My connection with them is reaffirmed in the kitchen and at the dinner table during our extended vacations back home.

My mother's recipe omits the ground peanuts that my father remembers from the early days. In my version of kare-kare, I reconcile the forgotten with the tried and true. My recipe is my tribute to the two people who, for good reasons, may no longer be in each other's lives, but who continue to be united in my memories of growing up in the Philippines and in the celebratory meals I serve to my own family. They taught me that in love, as in revolution, what matters is the regenerative power of making something your own. As a writer, I've come to realize that stories are the real soul food. Like taste memories, they are carried across continents and passed down from generation to generation to fortify the spirit. ◆

KARE-KARE

OXTAIL STEW IN THICK PEANUT SAUCE

PREPARATION TIME: 1 hour + 1½ hours to braise

YIELD: 4 servings

When preparing kare-kare, timing and organization are key, which is why the components of this recipe are subdivided, along with suggestions on when each component should be prepped. If you don't want to make the sautéed bagoong alamang, replace it with three tablespoons of fish sauce. See the Notes on page 111 for optional proteins beside oxtail.

OXTAIL

2 tablespoons annatto seeds (see Note on page 111; optional)

¼ cup vegetable oil

2 pounds oxtail

2 tablespoons all-purpose flour

½ onion, chopped

5 cups water

VEGETABLES

1 banana blossom, or 3 large artichoke hearts (not brined or marinated)

2 long or regular eggplants, cut into thick rounds

1 bunch long beans, trimmed and cut into 3-inch pieces, or 5 ounces green beans, trimmed

1 head bok choy, greens separated from stems, or spinach

SAUTÉED BAGOONG ALAMANG

½ onion, minced

2 cloves garlic, minced

1 large tomato, diced

¼ cup bagoong alamang (shrimp paste)

PEANUT SAUCE

2 tablespoons sweet rice powder, or ½ cup uncooked jasmine or sweet white rice, finely ground

1 tablespoon all-purpose flour

1 tablespoon cornstarch

1 tablespoon garlic powder

1 tablespoon onion powder

1 cup cold water

¼ cup toasted and roughly ground peanuts

3 tablespoons smooth peanut butter

4 tablespoons unsalted butter

SERVING

Cooked white or brown rice

Recipe continues >

KARE-KARE

continued

Some food historians have attributed kare-kare to Indian sepoys who came during the brief period of British occupation of the Philippines in the 1760s. Indians who intermarried with Filipinos and continue to be a small yet visible part of Philippine society most likely attempted to make their own dishes from back home using whatever local ingredients were at hand. Curry was perhaps indigenized into what we now know as kare-kare. Whatever its roots may be, what remains uncontested is that kare-kare is a staple in many celebratory occasions, and has become sariling atin, or our own.

Make the oxtail: Rinse the annatto seeds, if using, in water and pat dry. In a Dutch oven, heat the oil over medium-low heat until it shimmers. Add the seeds and fry, stirring frequently, for about 1 minute, or just until the oil turns red. Do not to let the oil boil. Strain the oil in a sieve, discard the seeds, and pour half of the flavored oil back into the pot. Reserve the other half of the oil for the peanut sauce.

Rinse the oxtail, pat dry, and then coat with the flour. Heat the pot of oil over high heat until the oil shimmers. Add the oxtail and sear for about 2 minutes on each side, or until browned all over. Pour the oil out of the pot and reserve for the bagoong. Leave the oxtail in the pot.

Add the onion and water to the pot. Bring the mixture to a boil over medium-high heat, then reduce the heat to medium-low. Simmer, covered, until the oxtail is tender, about 1 hour 20 minutes. If you prefer a falling-off-the-bone tenderness, add another 10 minutes.

While the oxtail simmers, make the vegetables: Bring a large pot of salted water to a boil over medium-high heat. Have this at the ready because the banana blossom will oxidize very quickly. Remove the blossom's stem and peel, then discard the red outer petals. Halve the beige center, and then quarter each half. Boil until tender, about 5 minutes. (If using artichoke hearts, let them boil for about 8 minutes.) Remove with a slotted spoon, drain, and set aside.

Add the eggplants to the salted water and boil for 3 to 5 minutes, until the middles begin to turn translucent. While the eggplants are boiling, prepare an ice-water bath by filling a large bowl half with ice cubes and half with water. Remove the eggplants with a slotted spoon and transfer to the ice-water bath for 1 minute. This will stop the cooking process and help them retain their color. Drain and set them aside with the banana blossom or artichoke hearts.

Repeat the same process for the long beans (boiling for about 3 minutes) and bok choy (boiling for about 2 minutes). The vegetables should be slightly tender but not overcooked. Tie the long beans into knots for easier handling.

While the oxtail continues to simmer, make the sautéed bagoong alamang: Heat the reserved oil (from searing the oxtail) in a small saucepan over medium heat until it shimmers. Add the onion and garlic and cook, stirring frequently, for 20 minutes, until they are caramelized. Add the tomato and bagoong alamang and cook until the mixture is fragrant and the moisture is gone, about 5 minutes. Remove from the heat and set aside.

About 10 minutes before the oxtail is done, make the peanut sauce: Combine the sweet rice powder, flour, cornstarch, garlic powder, and onion powder in a frying pan and cook over low heat, stirring frequently, until fragrant, about 2 minutes. Be careful not to burn this mixture or the sauce will have dark speckles. Transfer the toasted powder mixture to a bowl and stir in the water.

When the oxtails are done, transfer them to a plate and set them aside. Keep the broth simmering over low heat.

Pour about 2 tablespoons of the powder-water mixture at a time into the broth, until the desired smooth consistency is reached. Add the reserved half of the annatto oil.

Add the ground peanuts and peanut butter and stir until the soup base is creamy. If the sauce becomes too thick, thin it by adding water. Remove the soup base from the heat and add the butter, stirring until smooth. Then return the oxtail to the pot over low heat and simmer for about 5 minutes.

To assemble, ladle the stew into a soup tureen or clay pot. Arrange the boiled vegetables on top, with the fried bagoong alamang on the side. Serve with hot rice.

NOTES: If you don't have annatto seeds, you can instead take a large pinch of saffron and soak it in ¼ cup of warm water for 10 minutes. Use unflavored oil for searing the oxtail and cooking the bagoong, and add the saffron-flavored water to the pot when braising the meat.

Instead of oxtail, you can use beef (such as chuck or brisket), pork tail or hocks, chicken parts, seafood (such as monkfish), or tofu, but you'll need to adjust your simmering time accordingly. It will take about 60 minutes for beef or pork, 20 minutes for chicken, 10 minutes for seafood, and 5 minutes for tofu. If you use tofu, be sure to taste and season with salt as needed before serving.

Kare-Kare (page 109) >

CHAPTER 4

VEGETABLES

Vegetables are almost always cooked with seafood or bits of meat in Filipino cooking. Thus, traditional dishes are rarely purely vegetarian. One of the dishes in this chapter is the beloved pinakbet, aka pakbet, the name of which stems from the word *pinakebbet*, meaning "to cook till wrinkled." This indigenous dish from the Ilocos region is flavored with anchovy or shrimp paste. If scrimping is not required, pork or shrimp is also tossed in for good measure. Steaming and boiling of fresh native greens were norms of the land until two significant culinary introductions were adopted during the Spanish colonial period: guisa, from the Spanish word *guisar*, meaning "to sauté," and the tomato, brought to the country by way of the Galleon Trade. Eventually, garlic, onion, and tomato became the trifecta of sautés and the main flavor base of many a Filipino stew.

AMPALAYA EPIPHANY

DOWN THE ROAD FROM MY WORKPLACE, a nondescript Chinese restaurant serves a dish of bright, fresh bitter melon with black bean sauce over beef. I stop in there on those hectic days when a quick fix is needed. Even more than a comfort food, bitter melon—ampalaya— possesses anti-inflammatory properties, can strengthen immunity, and detoxifies the liver and blood. I also like ampalaya in munggo (mung beans), with lots of ginger, onion, and fistfuls of spinach. So whenever I begin to feel physically low, ampalaya is my go-to. Did my grandparents and great uncles bring this knowledge of ampalaya with them when they emigrated from the Philippines to the United States in 1927? Yes.

For me, because I received the loving inheritance of their knowledge, there is ritual and meditation infused in the way the bitter fruit that is ampalaya so poignantly continues to make its way into my kitchen.

My life partner, who was born and raised in Japan, added a layer to the ritual by teaching me about kirikata—the way of cutting—when preparing foods for various dishes. Among the handful of ways that I know, sogigiri, the angle-slicing cut, and usugiri, which means "thin cut," lend themselves well to ampalaya preparation, depending on whom I'm preparing it for. I have incorporated my knowledge of kirikata when serving ampalaya to friends less acquainted with its pungency. For example, with my scrambled eggs, I use usugiri. This way, the essence of its healthy but bold presence is manageable for newcomers, while also making it easy to marry the garlic, onion, and bitter melon flavors to

A third-generation Filipina American, LISA SUGUITAN MELNICK is a professor in the language arts and kinesiology divisions at the College of San Mateo, California. In 2015 her piece "Maség, An Artistic Tempest" won a Plaridel Award for Best Entertainment Story. Two of her pieces, "Agtawid" and "Out the Back Door," appear in *Beyond Lumpia, Pansit and Seven Manangs Wild*. She is the author of *#30 Collantes Street* and a contributing author for *Positively Filipino*. Lisa has been named one of the 100 Most Influential Filipina Women in the World (Global FWN100) by the Filipina Women's Network.

one another during sautéing. Becoming aware of the way of cutting has given me respect for the magnitude of my relationship with a fruit, which tethers me to my Ilocano roots. Ampalaya deserves to be dressed appropriately for each presentation; in this way, the recipients may also be invited to some sense of connection.

My favorite dish with ampalaya is pinakbet, a vegetable stew prepared in the simple and pure Ilocano style, the way my uncle Pepe taught me. Ampalaya is my comfort food when my heart longs for a visit to those childhood days when the family gathered every Thursday and Sunday; when my cousins and I watched the TV and tossed Grandma's throw pillows at one another across the room; when smelling the aromas of Uncle's food wafting from the nearby kitchen fortified our delicate third-generation ties to Philippine heritage.

Whenever I look down at my hand as it grasps the knife handle during food prep, I see my uncle's hands. I was always fascinated by the hands of my great-uncle, the brother of my grandfather. We called him Uncle Pepe, from his name, Epifanio—the Epiphany. I first learned how to cook ampalaya from him when I stayed in the home he shared with my grandparents in San Francisco's Richmond District during my college years. About his hands, I once wrote, "In contrast to Uncle Anong's hands, elephantine and bulbous at the fingertips, Uncle Pepe's mahogany hands—slender, tapered at the fingertips, long thumbs—are the masculine version of my own hands.... When he cooked, his hands adeptly created masterpieces: cutting, chopping, boiling, sautéing. Filleting, frittering, frying."

All this embodied memory I carried with me like an offering to my ancestors during my first journey to the Philippines at the age of 55. In a Silliman University café of all places, I discovered, like a virgin, ampalaya on its own—separated from its pinakbet partners—in scrambled eggs.

"Wow! Is that ampalaya in the eggs?!" I exclaimed in the breakfast line, up on tiptoes to lift myself above the glass to speak to the young man across the counter. The student server smiled first at my childlike thrill at his response of "Yes, ma'am" and then, to his offer of garlic rice on the side, laughed at my "Oh, my God, yes, please" enthusiasm.

He couldn't possibly know that my exclamations were prayers—prayers of gratitude for my epiphany: recognizing another exact moment when my ancestors decided to make their presence known on my first journey to the Philippines. To remind me that there was so much more they had to show me.

Before going to the Philippines, when I was not within the circle of my grandparents, cousins, aunties, and uncles, I experienced my Filipinaness as a token representation. I was a novelty in the California cities where we lived, granted a place at the table, the beloved brown one. I didn't realize how empty I had been—loving what others loved about me from the outside in, yet only vaguely aware of the void of love for myself from the inside out—until a journey to the ancestral homeland filled that half-empty vessel.

So, why is it that I identify a oneness with—of all foods—ampalaya?

1. It does not make nicey-nice to be accepted. People either love it or hate it, but its presence is strong and reliable.

2. Its prickly exterior demands tenacity in one's approach to discover and appreciate its specialness.

3. Even though it can play well with other veggies, as in pinakbet, it does just fine on its own, shining in its simplicity.

And here we are. ◆

Ampalaya >

TORTANG AMPALAYA

STIR-FRIED BITTER MELON OMELET

PREPARATION TIME: 10 minutes

YIELD: 4 servings

Ampalaya infuses yet another bold taste into the distinctive multi-flavor profile of Filipino dishes—bitterness. The vegetable is used in stews and stir-fries, its leaves in salads and soups. Believed to have medicinal merits, bitter melon was forced into the diets of Filipinos long ago by sautéing it with scrambled eggs. Here's an omelet version of the dish, delicious for breakfast, lunch, or dinner with garlic fried rice. Though I've had a longtime love of ampalaya—its flesh in pinakbet or stir-fries, its leaves in salad— enjoying it in eggs for breakfast was a first for me during that visit to Dumaguete in Negros Oriental. This simple discovery may seem small, but it symbolizes those many precious moments of revelation that one can't know what one doesn't yet know.

5 large eggs

2 teaspoons milk

Pinch fine salt

Pinch freshly ground black pepper

2 tablespoons vegetable oil

1 medium ampalaya, halved, seeded, and cut usugiri (into thin slices)

3 cloves garlic, minced

8 cherry tomatoes, halved

3 scallions, chopped and divided

———————————————

In a medium bowl, beat the eggs, milk, salt, and pepper and set aside.

Warm the oil in a large skillet over medium heat until it shimmers. Add the ampalaya and garlic and sauté until the garlic turns pale gold. Spread the mixture evenly all over the pan.

Pour the eggs over the sautéed ampalaya and garlic. Tilt the pan to spread the eggs evenly. Scatter the tomatoes on top, then most of the scallions, saving 1 tablespoon for garnish.

As the egg mixture begins to set, gently push the edges toward the center of the pan with a spatula, allowing the uncooked parts of the egg to run toward the outer edges of the pan. Do this two or three times, until the mixture is firm but still moist. Remove the skillet from the heat and cover it for 1 minute.

Garnish with the remaining 1 tablespoon scallions and serve.

ACROSS THE MILES

I LIE IN BED, wide awake, staring into the darkness. The noise from the window unit is deafening, but it is the only source of heat in my tiny efficiency apartment. Without a window in the bedroom, I can't tell if the sun has risen. It wouldn't make a difference anyway, since sleep has not been my friend for the past few weeks. My apartment is dark and empty. It's not easy adjusting to a new place, especially to a new country. Life is quieter in America. No street vendors' melodious call of "tahooo!"—a breakfast or in-between snack made of silken tofu and sugar syrup. No motorized tricycles with sidecars full of passengers whirring past on neighborhood streets. No screen doors loudly swinging shut or pots and pans clanging as breakfast is cooked in the kitchen. Nothing. Just the constant, obnoxiously loud window unit reminding me that I'm thousands of miles away from home.

I turn my head to check the digital clock on my bedside table. It's seven o'clock in the morning, around seven o'clock in the evening back home. My parents' New Year's Eve party would just be starting in the Philippines. While Christmas decorations in Manila are in full swing as soon as the months ending with "-ber" appear on the calendar, the holiday season could not be more absent in my new apartment. My walls and shelves are blank, empty, undecorated. Acknowledging the season is just too depressing when I'm so far from the people I love.

I was hired as an occupational therapist in rural Arkansas. Young, stubborn, and foolish, I naively leapt into what I thought was going to be the greatest adventure of my independent life. Nothing prepared me for the culture shock of moving to a small farming town in a dry

VANESSA LORENZO grew up in the Philippines, has lived in the United States since 2003, and is currently based in Virginia. On her website, AmusingMaria.com, she develops and features recipes, helping people with easy-to-cook dishes. She also writes about Filipino food and culture and life as an immigrant, with a focus on staying connected to her roots and sharing her Filipino heritage with the world. A case of wanderlust keeps her traveling to various locations locally and internationally. Her favorite response to every place she visits is "I could live here." Vanessa is also an occupational therapist who enjoys working with the elderly and helping them achieve their goals.

county. My vibrant city-girl world in the Philippines, driven by a packed social calendar, was thrown out the window. For the first time in my life, Christmas, my December birthday, and New Year's Eve—all huge family festivities—would be spent alone.

Each time I speak with my parents on the phone, I force myself to sound cheerful. Mom and Dad need to hear that I am all right, so I try hard to ease their worry about us living so far apart. Though tears ran down my face, my voice remains upbeat, masking my loneliness and longing to be back home.

The last time I spoke with Mom, she told me that all our relatives would be at our house for New Year's Eve. Every year, for as long as I could remember, my parents would host my birthday party along with the New Year's Eve celebration. It was a big event. Family and friends would come together, and the laughter and conversation were nonstop. I know that my relatives understand now, more than ever, that without the support and love from their children, it would be a hard New Year's Eve for my parents. My brother and his wife, who wants to further her studies, are set to move to San Francisco just a few months after I left.

I prepare myself mentally before calling home. This is going to be the hardest one, I think. I dial the number and, with all the cheer I can muster, greet my parents. "Happy New Year!" I explain I am calling early because work won't allow me to call them at midnight. Mom is thrilled to hear from me. After she excitedly gives me the details on the whos and whats of the party, she passes the phone to Dad, who asks, "How are ya?" in his trademark "American accent" picked up from the old cowboy movies he loves to watch. They sound happy, distracted, and busy. The party at our house is in full swing.

The cordless phone is passed from one relative to another, each asking, "How are you?" and wishing me "Happy Birthday! And Happy New Year!" They assure me they're taking care of my mom and dad. I hold the phone firmly to my ears and listen to the background noise of laughter, chitchat, and clinking of plates and utensils. It drowns out the buzzing of my window unit. I close my eyes and my small, dark room turns into our brightly lit house with Christmas lights strung around the tree.

I imagine my family all gathered around the long dining table filled with food; a tureen of our favorite piping-hot habichuelas, a white bean stew with pork and chorizo de bilbao, occupies center stage. I imagine them ladling their plates with generous servings of habichuelas over steamed white rice, the rich sauce coating the tender grains. I imagine some relatives asking for olive oil while some drizzle a teaspoon of patis and calamansi to top off the savory flavors of the stew. I imagine the stories being told about our family, the war our titos, titas, and grandparents had to endure, and our loved ones' jokes and bloopers being told over and over again while our family heirloom dish is eaten with gusto.

Eating habichuelas is as much genealogy as it is pleasure. Its history in our family dates back to a man from Leon, Spain—Constantino Gonzales, or Lolo Constantino, my great-grandfather. A soldier assigned to the Philippines, he met my great-grandmother, Lola Dominga, the love of his life, and decided never to leave the country. Habichuelas, a dish he grew up eating, became a mainstay meal in their household every Sunday. My aunts, young children at the time, remember their grandfather pouring olive oil over the beans and rice with gusto. Back then, the stew was flavored with tocino viejo, a homemade salt-and-peppered pork fatback, air-dried for several days. Now, chorizo de bilbao, ham, or bone-in pork meat, and the preferred seasoning of fish sauce with freshly squeezed calamansi enhance the taste of habichuelas.

Unlike her sisters, my mother missed out on the privileged Spanish-Filipino life. She was born during World War II, when her parents and sisters, along with an elderly Lolo Constantino and Lola Dominga, had to flee their ancestral home to escape from Japanese soldiers wanting to take them as hostages. Assisted by Filipino guerrillas, they sought refuge in a district in the Philippines called Barrio San Antonio. While

My family's heirloom dish has been on every dining table where my relatives have gathered. It is in the center of a lot of laughter, storytelling, gossip sessions, and even crying sessions when those who have passed away, those who have moved away, and those who have fallen ill are remembered.

in hiding, their hometown of Tumauini burned to the ground, and the family's home and everything in it was lost. I would like to think that habichuelas sustained the family while they rebuilt their lives after the war. With just a few economical ingredients, this simple yet hearty meal nourished bodies and souls through the years.

My mom taught me as a young girl how to cook habichuelas. The memory is vivid. She is standing in front of a two-burner stove, the kind where a rubber tube connects the burners to a tank of Gasul. With a spatula in one hand, a plate on the other, she systematically adds chopped garlic, onions, and tomatoes to the pan before her, pausing between each ingredient to make sure it cooks well so the flavors are released into the hot oil. She talks while sautéing, and the sounds of the pan sizzling and spatula scraping accompany her voice. The flavorful aroma of the ingredients saturates the screened kitchen while I learn that mashing the tomatoes in the oil with the onions and garlic is an important step to flavor the habichuelas. The navy beans are simmering in broth on the other burner. Mom lifts the lid to check if the beans are tender and, in one swoop, ladles a scoop of beans and broth into the pan with the onions, garlic, and tomatoes. The steam it creates melts the caramelized ingredients. She then mashes the beans into the mixture and creates a thickened red-orange sauce, which is then poured back into the pot with the navy beans.

Over the years, several of my contemporaries moved to other countries or other parts of the Philippines. The third and fourth generations of our close-knit family scattered. We still have get-togethers full of love and lively camaraderie, but they are less frequent now, and the number of attendees has dwindled. However, good memories bind those who remember the outings, parties, and picnics back home. Stories of our heritage and our experiences of moving to other locations will hopefully be passed on. I hope our recipe of habichuelas thrives in our new worlds and is handed down to younger generations long after we are gone.

My family's heirloom dish has been on every dining table where my relatives have gathered. It is in the center of a lot of laughter, storytelling, gossip sessions, and even crying sessions when those who have passed away, those who have moved away, and those who have fallen ill are remembered. The saying "Nothing lasts forever" is true. Children grow and adults wither, but our habichuelas, the simple and humble bean stew that's fed my family for generations wherever we may be, has proven itself to be hardy. Originating from Spain, it sailed across the Atlantic and Pacific Oceans, was cooked and eaten for years in a remote province in the Philippines, withstood two world wars, and has now traveled the world with every member of the family who knows the recipe by heart. I hope it continues to live on the same way our memories and stories do.

I open my eyes and I am back in my dark, drab apartment. No rays of light or sounds of life stream into my bedroom. Only memories. Inspiring and heartwarming memories of habichuelas from across the miles, comforting me and replacing my sadness with the promise of continuity and a hope for a better future. I say my goodbyes, hang up the phone, and get ready for work. ◆

HABICHUELAS

NAVY BEANS WITH CHORIZO AND TOMATO CHUTNEY

PREPARATION TIME: 30 minutes + 2 hours to soak
COOKING TIME: 2 hours
YIELD: 6–8 servings

This habichuelas recipe is a highly modified version of our heirloom recipe. I made it more versatile: it can be eaten hot or cold, with or without rice or bread, or as a topping for green salads. Here, anchovies and chorizo de bilbao flavor the chopped stewed tomatoes, which are cooked and reduced to a chutney. This is used as a topping for the navy beans, instead of the traditional recipe of stewing the beans in tomato sauce. Much as in the narrative, a condiment of fish sauce with calamansi or lemon juice, or olive oil, or both complement the dish well.

BEANS

1 pound pork riblets, cut into individual ribs

1 (2.5-ounce) chorizo de bilbao or other smoked sausage, such as kielbasa

5 cups dry navy beans, rinsed, soaked for 2 hours, and drained

10 cups water

1 onion, quartered

1 tablespoon coarse sea salt

TOMATO CHUTNEY

2 tablespoons olive oil

1 ½ tablespoons finely chopped onion

3 tablespoons minced garlic

1 (2-ounce) can anchovies, drained and finely chopped

2 (14-ounce) cans diced tomatoes, drained

½ teaspoon coarse sea salt

½ teaspoon freshly ground black pepper

¼ teaspoon granulated sugar

1 teaspoon fish sauce (optional)

GARNISH (OPTIONAL)

12 ounces bacon, fried until crisp

1 bunch flat-leaf parsley, chopped

Make the beans: Combine the riblets, chorizo, beans, water, onion, and salt in a large pot. Bring the mixture to a boil over medium-high heat. Reduce the heat to medium-low, cover, and simmer for about 1 ½ hours, or until the beans are fork tender. Remove the chorizo from the stew and cut it into small cubes. Set it aside to use for the tomato chutney.

Transfer the beans and riblets to a serving dish and set aside.

Recipe continues >

HABICHUELAS

continued

Make the tomato chutney: Heat the oil in a skillet over medium-low heat until it shimmers. Add the onion and cook, stirring occasionally, until translucent, about 3 minutes. Mix in the garlic and cook for about 30 seconds. Mix in the reserved chorizo, anchovies, and tomatoes and cook, stirring occasionally, for 3 minutes. Add the salt, pepper, and sugar and mix well.

Reduce the heat to low. Mash the chorizo-tomato mixture gently with a spatula. Cook, stirring occasionally, until the mixture reduces and thickens. Add the fish sauce, if using, for extra flavor. Remove the chutney from the heat.

To serve, ladle the habichuelas with the pork riblets into bowls and spoon the chutney on top, or mix it in. Garnish with the bacon and parsley, if using, and serve hot.

NOTE: Serve the habichuelas on its own or with steamed rice. You can also refrigerate it and serve as a bean salad or as a topping for green salads (excluding the pork riblets).

YOU CAN'T RUSH A GOOD THING

"**A**RE YOU READY?!" Tatay, my grandpa, asked as I snapped on my seat belt in his 1980s Isuzu.

He was late. Again.

I waited a lot after school. Most kids got out of class and their parents were right outside the door, ready to take them home. I was the last to be picked up sometimes. No, actually—a lot of times. I waved goodbye to my classmates and watched my teachers leave campus, each face riddled with pity. Eventually, the school's office secretary had to fetch me so that I could make a phone call home back in her office, which smelled of old pencil shavings and brittle Bible pages. After a few minutes, Tatay would be in front of the school and I would be thrilled to see him.

He had slicked-back black hair with a handsome Pleasantville side part, a style that never left him since he first adopted it in his younger years. He wore a neatly tucked-in button-down shirt under his tan Members Only jacket. And the best part of his look? A big, wide smile that poured out happiness—even if he did forget to put in his dentures.

Tatay brought me to and from school every day. Our routine was the same every morning: he waited for me as I changed into my hideous green plaid jumper uniform and as I ate the very adult almusal, or breakfast, that my grandma Inang made me: traditional pan de sal rolls and sharp instant coffee to dip the pieces of bread in. We got in the car and drove to my Catholic school at Top of the Hill along Mission Street, I gave him a kiss on the cheek, and I headed to my class. A lot of the time I was late, too. We never abided by the 8:25 a.m. to 3:00 p.m. rules.

JOANNE BOSTON-KWANHULL is a Filipino food advocate and social media/digital coordinator in the San Francisco Bay Area. She is creative director of JBKollaborations, through which she assists with the promotion of local and national Filipino food events. In 2016, Joanne was recognized as one of the top 10 young Filipino Americans in the United States by the Philippine Embassy and chosen to be part of the Filipino American Young Leaders Program (FYLPRO). In 2015, she became a founding board member of the Filipino Food Movement (FFM), a nonprofit organization. She was a planning board member for Savor Filipino, the first Filipino food festival in the United States, in 2014 and 2016. Her writing has appeared on the CBS San Francisco website, the *San Francisco Chronicle*, and others. Joanne is currently a full-time communication sciences student and a medical oncology reimbursement specialist.

No, we were there at 8:35 a.m. and left at 3:15 p.m. Or, more often than not, 8:45 a.m. and 3:30 p.m.

Tatay and I were a team. He brought me to the corner store, where he bought me Juicy Fruit gum. I chewed so much of it as a child, my teeth enamel eroded. Off to the dentist I went in Tatay's car, and he waited for me to get silver caps on all eight of my front teeth. Come to think of it, I don't think we were always on time for those appointments either. He waited for me to finish watching *Heathcliff* cartoons, or I waited for him to finish watching *Bonanza*. We waited for each other and we were cool with that. We enjoyed each other's company.

Tatay used to travel back and forth between San Francisco and Umingan in Pangasinan; however, the time came that, due to his health and age, my family thought it was best for him and Inang to remain in their homeland—back in the home they built together, where a giant jackfruit tree welcomed visitors to the house made of wood, with first-floor windows safeguarded by intricate iron cages. Inside, Tatay and Inang waited with arms wide open for anyone who came through the door.

It took 10 years before I came through their door. Between 1997 and 2007, I had a severe Philippines drought. Not one visit. It was a long time to wait.

I let time pass by until it hit me: *What the hell was I waiting for?* I returned to Umingan with my mom and sister for Tatay and Inang's 83rd birthday party. I also went back a couple of years later, this time bringing my boyfriend. By the end of the trip, that boyfriend would be my fiancé.

When it was time, my aunts added the mung beans, a bit of water, maybe some fish-tinged patis or bagoong for that funky I-don't-know-what. And then we waited . . . and waited . . . and waited . . . for what seemed to be the longest 30 to 45 minutes of my life.

He asked Inang and Tatay for their blessing. It was one of the happiest moments of my life to see them smile and nod their heads in agreement. A girl waits for this moment her whole life, and I am lucky to have shared it with them.

Many wonderful memories of that trip stand out, and one of them is balatong, or mung beans, also known nationally as monggo. My aunts prepared and served it to us in the kitchen of my grandparents' provincial house. We ate so much of it during our visit, my husband now claims it is his favorite Filipino dish. Our memories of the dish, however, are not just of eating it, but also of preparing it.

In 90°F heat, my muumuu-clad aunts cooked balatong to the tune of melancholic 1990s Tagalog love songs. Minced garlic, slices of fresh pork belly butchered at sunrise at the town's wet market with layers of fat and meat caramelizing into golden chunks, and slivered petite red onions picked from the family's crops danced in a paryok, or clay pot, atop a propane-fueled stove. My little cousin, who was assigned to harvest greens, ran outside to fulfill his task as the swaying malunggay, or moringa, tree in our backyard begged for its glorious deep green oval leaves to be picked.

Off to the side of our royal blue–tiled kitchen sink, the unassuming mung beans soaked in a pink plastic basin. Meanwhile, the aromatics in the paryok melted and developed flavor—or lasa, as we call it—that inspiring sensation on the palate, inviting you to eat more. I looked at the walls: peeling bright teal paint and tiny lizards defying gravity. I wondered what other ulam, or dishes, my grandma and aunts prepared within these walls: lauya, adobo, and, probably, sinigang. And I also wondered if our reptilian guardians longed to have a taste of these creations.

When it was time, my aunts added the mung beans, a bit of water, maybe some fish-tinged patis or bagoong for that funky I-don't-know-what. And then we waited . . . and waited . . . and waited . . . for what seemed to be the longest 30 to 45 minutes of my life. Every now and then I sneaked a peek into the pot of molten bubbling mass, impatiently willing for that desired thick and velvety consistency to happen—when the contents within the tiny beans collectively lent a beautiful starchiness to the fragrant broth that enveloped them earlier.

My little cousin returned with the bounty from our tree. My aunts divvied up the malunggay bunches of floss-thin branches and plucked off the hundreds of tiny leaves. When the time came, the leaves were thrown into the pot and quickly wilted upon contact with the soup. The balatong was ready.

My aunt beckoned me to her side and served me a bowl of rice. She slowly poured a ladle full of balatong over the rice, which I mixed together into a hearty mash speckled with beans, white rice, red tomatoes, and pork. Each grainy bite perfect, summoning sweat to the brow, aligning with the exhausting humidity of the Pangasinan air. Now *that*, my friends, is home. Comfort. Something worth waiting for. All the work. All the effort. All the waiting. That first bite is as satisfying and warm as my grandfather's hug. The waiting: it's worth it.

In May 2010, Tatay passed away. I still can't believe he's gone. After his death, I was full of regret. *I wish I spent more time with him. I wish I didn't get him mad all the time. I wish I hadn't waited that long to see him again.* I can only wish that I made him proud in the 26 years he knew me. And Tatay, I still don't abide by the 8:25 a.m. rule. Yup, I'm still late to everything and usually have coworkers waiting for me in the morning. I'm working on it. With that said, some things are worth waiting for . . . like stews, hugs, and a grinning grandfather at your school ready to take you home. ◆

MONGGO {BALATONG}

STEWED MUNG BEANS WITH PORK BELLY SOFRITO

Inang taught Mom how to cook and Mom taught me how to cook. Not only did I learn how to measure ingredients using old-world Philippine techniques instead of standard measuring implements, I also learned that patience, especially in stews like balatong, is important. Equally important to know is that time only goes forward, and it is up to the cook to manage her time efficiently. This version of balatong uses spinach instead of malunggay because it is more readily available, although my mom sometimes uses ampalaya (bitter melon) leaves instead. She has also been known to use chicken in place of the pork, and to add eggplant for variety. Any way I have it, I still count it as my favorite ulam! It's great served over steamed white rice.

PREPARATION TIME: 45 minutes

YIELD: 6–8 servings

12 ounces dried split mung beans

1 pound thinly sliced pork belly

3–5 cloves garlic, minced

1 large white onion, chopped

2 Roma tomatoes, chopped

Salt and freshly ground black pepper, to taste

1 tablespoon soy sauce, plus more to taste

2 teaspoons chicken bouillon, plus more to taste

8 ounces baby spinach

Crumbled chicharron (pork rind), for garnish (optional)

Chopped scallions, for garnish (optional)

Put the mung beans in a medium saucepan and add enough water to cover them by 1 inch. Bring the water to a boil over medium heat, then remove the pan from the heat and cover it.

Warm a large pot over medium-high heat. Place a single layer of the sliced pork belly in the pot, taking care not to crowd it; you may need to cook the pork belly in a few batches. Cook the pork belly until it is golden and crispy and the fat has rendered. Transfer the pork belly to a plate lined with paper towels and remove and discard all but 2 tablespoons of the pork fat from the pot.

Add the garlic and cook over medium-high heat until aromatic, about 1 minute. Add the onion and cook, stirring occasionally, until translucent, about 2 minutes. Add the tomatoes, season with salt and pepper, and scrape the bottom of the pot to loosen the golden bits left by the pork. Return the pork belly to the pot and add the soy sauce and chicken bouillon. Cook until the tomatoes have released their juices and a thick sauce forms, about 3 minutes.

Add the boiled mung beans. Stir to combine thoroughly, reduce the heat to medium, and cook the mixture until the beans are done. If you like a thinner stew, add water to achieve your desired consistency.

Right before serving, add the spinach. Taste and add salt, pepper, bouillon, and/or soy sauce as needed. Garnish with chicharron and scallions, if using, and serve.

DRIVING HOME

THE FAINT SOUND of a slamming door resonated in the almost-empty parking lot of the schist-clad building of 112 Parnell. I hurriedly locked the back door of the restaurant as the alarm I activated inside beeped.

Walking toward my car, I was oblivious to the acrid scent that lingered on me from the day's work in the kitchen. A wave of exhaustion washed over me as soon as I got behind the wheel. I checked my watch; it was half past two in the morning. I had clocked in 19½ hours of work.

When I switched on the car radio, Adele's voice ripped the silence with "Send My Love (To Your New Lover)." The song kept me company as I navigated the road. That early Saturday morning, the horizon glowed with different hues from the lights of skyscrapers amid the gleaming moonlit sky.

It had been barely seven weeks since my big move from the pastoral plains of Hurunui to the populous city of Auckland. Thanks to the massive signage leading south of the motorway toward Hamilton, where I lived, I knew I was heading in the right direction.

Between the beaming lights of passing cars, my thoughts slipped back to the kitchen. The restaurant had not yet opened, but it felt already full-on. There was plenty of running, stirring, scraping, and cutting. Clattering of pots and pans, clinking of forks and spoons, spluttering of hot oil, and boiling of water accompanied the deafening sound of the running exhaust. Everything had been orchestrated and rehearsed. Things were running as a healthy kitchen should.

LEONARDO ESPERACION FERNANDEZ JR. worked as a veterinarian in the Philippines and a pig farmer in rural New Zealand before moving to Auckland to focus on a career in the restaurant business and becoming a full-fledged chef. He was the runner-up of *MasterChef New Zealand* 2015.

Leo grew up in the town of Laoac in Pangasinan, a northern province of the Philippines. Raised with his two siblings, Ely and Mark, by his Ilocano father and Ilonga mother, he was exposed to good, passionate cooking from an early age. Leo's food philosophy is "acknowledge and stick to the roots and cook from the heart." He believes that Filipino cuisine is beautiful in itself and deserves better recognition from the rest of world.

A draft of cold air crept inside the car, shaking me out of my reverie. The song playing on the radio transitioned to a beat more unfamiliar and desolate. Traffic flowed easily, and I exited toward East Tamaki. It was an easy drive through a motorway that, at regular hours, was congested with traffic jams.

Almost home to Flat Bush, and finally a bit decompressed from the day, I realized how hungry I was. I had eaten only a piece of flatbread and teaspoons of various sauces, broths, and pastes the whole day. I squeezed my car between two others already parked on the side of the road and checked my watch again. It was 3:10 a.m.

I quietly unlocked the door, so as not to waken my snoring flatmates, and hurried straight to the fridge. Famished, I grabbed a bowl of leftovers and placed it in the microwave. But this was not just leftovers; this was pinakbet. The pungent aroma of the mixed vegetable stew teased my nostrils when I peeled back the plastic wrap. At last, my first decent meal of the day. Coming home was soothing. And when home is away from home, eating a dish that reminds you of it is comfort without measure.

Growing up in a typical Ilocano household in the northern province of the Philippines, I had discovered one of my all-time favorite dishes, pinakbet, at a young age. It was prepared by Inang Rosa, my great-grandmother. Her interpretation of the dish started with pork collar. She prepared the meat and braised it adobo style with annatto until it was really tender before prepping the myriad of vegetables for the pinakbet. The smell of garlic, onion, and tomato dissipated from her paryok as she sautéed them with her wooden ladle. She scooped out the pork, which almost pulled apart, and added it to the sauté. As a child, I thought that the scent of frying pork was heaven. Next, eggplant, okra, bitter melon, and patani (lima beans) hit the pot, finished off with bagoong (fermented fish paste) poured through a fine sieve and rinsed down with hot water. After pressing the residue from the bagoong with the ladle, she covered the pot, leaving it to cook away in the dalikan, or earthen stove, while she attended to her other chores. When she returned, her shriveled, strong hands gave the paryok a gentle shake.

"Mangan tayon!" she called out. Let's eat!

We never doubted her skills. Her pinakbet was perfect every time.

Inang imparted to us the legacies of her love and unselfishness as she shared her passion for food. My mom, a true Ilonggo (a person from Iloilo, the southern part of the Philippines) by blood, was one of the many recipients. Mom's rendition of pinakbet, however, is slightly different. She adds kadyos (pigeon peas) and simplifies the process by sautéing the pork belly and rendering its fat. This version, just like Inang's, is second to none.

During my university days, I looked forward to semester breaks, when I would return to the comfort of family and food. The commute from the university to home took eight hours. But it was worth it. Mama welcomed my homecoming with a beautifully set table and a dish of pinakbet. I long for pinakbet to this day, perhaps just like anybody who has chosen the path of becoming an immigrant.

When I decided to leave home, I had to teach myself how to cook. I learned the basics of cookery, learned to recreate food I grew up with, and learned to adapt food to my new location. It was more than just a human need. It filled the gaps when I felt lacking. It changed my life.

My deep connection with food led me to veer off my original career path. I went from veterinarian to swine farmer, then to chef and restaurateur in this foreign land I now consider my second home. As I devoured every morsel of pinakbet the bowl contained, I thought about the next chapter of my so-called destiny. Most likely, I'd be driving these roads of Auckland for years to come—probably at the same odd restaurateur hours as I did tonight. But all I really knew was this: my memories of food—like those evoked by my humble pinakbet—inspire me and reconnect me to my past, to my heritage, and to my culture. Like the massive road signs I follow on the motorway, my memories of food have a way of reassuring me and keeping me on the right track. Amid the darkness and uncertainty, they serve as my reference point, my compass, and help me navigate this road I chose to take in food, no matter how long and winding it turns out to be. ◆

PINAKBET AT BAGNET

MIXED VEGETABLES WITH BAGOONG
SAUCE AND CRISPY PORK BELLY

PREPARATION TIME: 1 ½ hours + 1 hour to braise

YIELD: 6 servings

Pinakbet is a popular vegetable stew originating from the Ilocos region in the northern part of the Philippines. A special version is enriched with bagnet, also known as lechon, kawali, or crispy fried pork belly. Authentic Ilocano pinakbet uses a few key ingredients: tomato, eggplant, bitter melon, and okra seasoned with fermented fish sauce, or bagoong isda. With the influx of Filipinos and other Asian immigrants to New Zealand, an increasing number of growers have found a market for these more exotic vegetables. It has become much easier to recreate the authentic dishes of my childhood since I moved here in 2008. Look first in an Asian market. If you can't find all the ingredients, I have included substitutions that will work well.

SAUCE

2 tablespoons vegetable oil

3 cloves garlic, minced

½ cup chopped onion

2 tomatoes, chopped

¼ cup bagoong (preferably bagoong monamon, fermented anchovies)

1 ½ cups water

VEGETABLES

4–6 Asian eggplants, or 1 medium eggplant, thinly sliced

1 medium bitter melon, halved lengthwise, seeded, and thinly sliced

2 medium zucchinis, thinly sliced

2 tomatoes, thinly sliced

3 tablespoons vegetable oil

Salt and freshly ground black pepper, to taste

BAGNET

1 pound pork belly, sliced

1 medium onion, chopped

2 bay leaves

3 cloves garlic, crushed

1 tablespoon coarse sea salt

Vegetable oil, for frying

ASSEMBLY

1 ½ cups frozen pigeon peas or green peas, blanched and smashed

1 pound okra, boiled in salted water for 3 minutes

Recipe continues >

Preheat the oven to 375°F.

Make the sauce: Heat the oil in a medium sauté pan over medium heat until it shimmers. Add the garlic and onion and cook, stirring occasionally, until the onion is translucent, about 3 minutes. Add the tomatoes and sauté for 3 minutes. Spoon in the bagoong through a sieve, then pour in the water through the sieve. Simmer the mixture for 5 minutes, then remove it from the heat and set it aside to cool to room temperature.

Pour the cooled sauce into a food processor or blitz with a stick blender until the sauce is well blended. Spread the sauce in the bottom of a 10 × 10-inch baking dish.

Make the vegetables: Arrange alternating slices of eggplant, bitter melon, zucchini, and tomato in the sauced baking dish, starting at the outer edge of the dish and working concentrically toward the center. Overlap the slices a little to display the colors. Drizzle the vegetables with the vegetable oil and season with salt and pepper as needed.

Cover the vegetables with a piece of parchment paper cut to fit inside the dish. Bake until the vegetables are roasted and tender, about 45 minutes. Reduce the oven temperature to 350°F.

While the vegetables bake, make the bagnet: Combine the pork belly, onion, bay leaves, garlic, and salt in a 2-quart saucepan. Add enough water to cover the ingredients and simmer over low heat for about 1 hour, or until the pork is tender.

Drain the pork and transfer it to a small roasting pan. Bake for 30 to 45 minutes, until the pork has dried.

In a 12-inch frying pan, heat 2 inches of oil over medium-high heat until a deep-fry thermometer registers 375°F to 400°F. Add the pork in a single layer and deep-fry until crispy and golden brown, 5 to 10 minutes. Transfer the pork to paper towels to drain. Chop the pork into small pieces.

Assemble: Divide the smashed pigeon peas among six plates. Fan out the vegetables on the pigeon peas in a circular pattern. Arrange the pork belly and okra in the middle of the vegetables. Spoon more sauce over all and serve.

COOKING BY HINDSIGHT

A five-time Palanca Award winner in English poetry, FRANCIS C. MACANSANTOS (1949–2017) won the National Commission for Culture and the Arts (NCCA) Writers' Prize for Poetry in 2003. He published four books of poetry: *The Words and Other Poems*; *Womb of Water, Breasts of Earth*; *Balsa: Poemas Chabacano*; and *Snail Fever: Poems of Two Decades*. *Snail Fever* was a Philippine National Book Award winner for poetry in English in 2017 and *Balsa* was a Philippine National Book Award finalist in 2012. He taught at several universities, and served on panels of critics in creative writing workshops throughout the Philippines. In 2014, Francis was one of the winners of the Maria W. Faust Sonnet Contest. He and his wife, writer/mathematician Priscilla Macansantos, raised their daughter, the writer Monica Macansantos, in Baguio City, Philippines, and Delaware.

ALTHOUGH AS A CHILD, I did make occasional stops in the kitchen area, where I found myself making desultory observations, at times even to admire the array of ingredients, the marshaling of it all—one might say the orchestration—cooking was a matter of absolute indifference to me. Mother was a great cook under whose spell the simplest dishes turned unfailingly delectable. Spoiled as a señor was I, whose interest remained in the domain of the dinner table.

Leaving home for university didn't bring me any closer to cooking experience, either. I relied on the campus cafeteria and the occasional carinderia, or eatery, no matter how much I missed home cooking. It wasn't until I started teaching at the Mindanao State University in Marawi in the late 1970s, with the Mindanao Moro insurgency arguably still at its fiercest, that I learned to fry and sauté and make simple soups. Where I roomed at the bachelors' quarters was a long walk away from the nearest eatery, and the trek, particularly at night, was especially risky. Sudden bursts of gunfire were not uncommon in the area. Those who lived where I did had learned to cook to survive.

But then I fell into a company of cooks—virtual chefs—who lived there and taught hotel and restaurant management only a few blocks down the hill. In the first few weeks of my arrival in the university, to dispel the gloom of not being able to venture out at night, together with a guitarist friend, I had regaled (or was it pestered?) the occupants of the single women's dorm (adjacent to my dorm) with rambunctious renderings of the Beatles, Chuck Berry, Elvis, and so on. In gratitude for my services, the chefs in my audience offered to cook for me for a very modest fee. I had virtually sung for my supper. But that left an incipient cooking career in limbo. Rock stars, beware!

The year after ushered a newcomer into our midst who taught political science. He was as handsome as debonair, and boasted various sterling credentials. He had been a varsity soccer player, a speechwriter for a labor leader, a former classmate of presidential daughter (and later president in her own right) Gloria Macapagal, a green-card holder, a photojournalist, and, most importantly for the bachelors with deprived palates, a cook with the most unique experience: he had once been a cook for his comrades in the New People's Army (the Philippines' Communist Party rebel army)! With him around, I felt truly like a privileged trooper. I watched him cook—and I ate with gusto. How lucky the rebels had been!

I did not begin to cook regularly until I got married to a Baguio-born Ilocana in 1980 and migrated to that mountain city a year later to join her there. Blessed as I had also been with a great cook for a mother who did all the cooking, my wife never saw the need to learn. She might have learned to cook on her own later, but I came into her life. Too, being underpaid teachers under martial law, we couldn't complain. Eating out was not prohibited but outright prohibitive. When her mom left for America, I had to step into her place. Necessity was mother now. And so I cooked.

Northern Philippine cuisine is in the main truly unique. It is breathlessly different, as anyone from anywhere else in the islands would testify. First of all, unlike most of the Christianized, westernized edibles that abound, it is never a slave to the tomato. A guisa, or sauté, with this fruit

Northern Philippine cuisine is in the main truly unique. It is breathlessly different, as anyone from anywhere else in the islands would testify.

or vegetable would be an anomaly to the truly Ilocano palate. It may be a guest garnish in pinakbet, but that would be only as a concession, to show that a foreigner, too, is welcome. This was once demonstrated to me with much calm finesse by my father-in-law (in one of his rare visits from California), who said as he cooked, "You can also add on some slices of tomato toward the end of cooking, like so." Pinakbet, he also explained, has less sauce than dinendeng, which is nearly a soup dish.

To my surprise, in my mountain nook in Baguio at the very beginnings of my domesticity, the cooks I once had known came to my aid like ministering angels. Memories of cooking rose from the past somewhat à la recherche but in reverse. People and places culled the memories of food and cooking. Some, though partial and incomplete recipes, only had to be filled in like jigsaw puzzles. Blessed be the culinary unconscious! A recipe I retrieved from the subliminal realm is that of my mother-in-law's Ilocos Sur dinendeng. But this is slightly modified with the use of yellow camote, or sweet potato, instead of red squash. Too, for health reasons (I suffer from gout), I avoid fermented fish sauce and use red wine (a less virulent alternative) in its stead. Not infusing into an Ilocano dish that food base, which is no less than fish bagoong, is nearly like not having water in a Saharan sojourn.

Fortunately for me, dinendeng is a dish with the subtlest flavors, with nearly the entire array of the backyard vegetables providing variety to its final statement of theme, such that the motif that emerges depends on the arrangement, which no bass fiddle (even if food base) can tug down from under. Bagoong, in Ilocos Sur country, is more catalyst than food base. ◆

DINENDENG

MIXED VEGETABLE AND SHRIMP STEW WITH RED WINE

PREPARATION TIME: 20 minutes

YIELD: 4 servings

Dinendeng is a lightly flavored dish, nuanced by the very variety of its composition. It needs the flavor of the sea, though, and of the earth, to lend it some gravitas, though never to tie it down. Bagoong is the ideal potion that fulfills such a task. In this particular version, however, shrimp supplies the marine element, and red wine the earthiness.

2 medium sweet potatoes (preferably yellow), peeled and chopped

½ pound medium to large head-on shrimp (preferably white)

1 medium onion, finely chopped

1 (1-inch) piece ginger, peeled and sliced

3 tablespoons dry red wine

1 (5-ounce) bunch string beans, stringed and cut into 1-inch pieces

6–12 winged beans or sugar snap peas, stringed and halved lengthwise

12 okra, halved crosswise

12 squash blossoms, calyxes removed and stalks peeled

Salt and freshly ground black pepper, to taste

Combine the sweet potatoes, shrimp, onion, ginger, and wine in a large wok. Add enough water so that the wok is about a third of the way full (about 3 cups). Bring to a simmer over low heat, then cover. Simmer for about 5 minutes, or until the sweet potatoes are cooked but still firm. Transfer the sweet potatoes and shrimp to separate plates. Remove and discard the heads and shells of the shrimp. Set the shrimp aside.

Add the string beans and winged beans to the wok. Cover, raise the heat to high, and bring the broth to a rolling boil. Boil for about 3 minutes, then add the okra, cover, and cook for about 3 minutes, or until the okra is tender but still vibrant green. Add the squash blossoms, cover, and cook for 1 to 2 more minutes. Taste and add salt and pepper as needed.

Return the sweet potatoes and shrimp to the wok and boil for a few seconds. Serve hot.

CHAPTER 5

NOODLES

PERHAPS THE MOST discernible gift of the Chinese to Filipino cuisine is noodles. Unlike pasta that comes in different shapes and forms, Filipino noodles are principally long and stringlike, or they are square or round wrappers used for dumplings or egg rolls. This chapter features pansit (or pancit), the noodle dish commonly brought to potlucks and prepared for birthday celebrations. While the name has become a blanket term for Filipino-style stir-fried rice noodles, there are a variety of pansit dishes, such as pansit palabok (aka pansit mala-bon), rice noodles topped with a thick shrimp sauce, and pansit molo, a dumpling soup.

THE PRICE OF FREEDOM

M Y FATHER WANTED to murder someone when he saw a skeletal version of his daughter walking toward him. It was just two weeks
after he and my mother had dropped me off at the Kalayaan (Freedom)
Residence Hall of the University of the Philippines (UP) Diliman, where
I began my life as a college student.

I had known that one of the first things I would miss about living
with my parents in Baguio was my father's cooking. I wanted my freedom, and for this I had to forgo the comforts of home. But I didn't expect
my homesickness to manifest itself as an acute physical revulsion as I
tasted the food they served us at the dorm cafeteria. The meat tasted old
and strange, the rice was lumpy and unevenly cooked, and they never
seemed to care if the lumps of hard pork they served in an unidentifi-
able orange sauce were undercooked.

My father, a poet/writer, had always been the cook in our family, having come from a family of cooks. My mother, who met him in her early
20s, became so spoiled by his cooking that she never felt the need to
match his skills in the kitchen. I was an only child who grew up eating
well, since I had a father who made daily trips to the Baguio Market for
fresh vegetables, fish, and meat. He was a finicky Zamboangueño[1] who
preferred to clean out the very last entrails of a fish and rinse salad vegetables more than once and would never, ever reuse cooking oil. At the
Baguio Market, or at the smaller talipapa, or wet market, in Engineer's

---

1 a person from Zamboanga, a region on the southern island of Mindanao

MONICA
MACANSANTOS was
born and raised in the
Philippines and holds
an MFA in writing
from the Michener
Center for Writers
at the University of
Texas at Austin. Her
work has appeared in
Day One, *The Masters
Review*, *Longform
Fiction*, *Thin Noon*,
Aotearotica, and *TAYO
Literary Magazine*,
among other places.
She recently had work
recognized in the No-
table List of *The Best
American Essays 2016*,
edited by Jonathan
Franzen. Monica lives
in Wellington, New
Zealand, where she
is pursuing a PhD in
creative writing at
Victoria University's
International Institute
of Modern Letters.

Hill that was closer to our home, he had designated sukis, the vendors he was loyal to, for almost every kind of meat: chicken, fish, steak,
tuna. He would buy rice only from a Chinese man from Hong Kong at
the talipapa who also sold the freshest eggs, or from another Chinese
dry-goods merchant at the Baguio Market who would run her fingers
through a mountain of jasmine rice at the entrance to her stall, boast-
ing that the grains of her rice were whole and not broken into pieces.
As I grew older, my father would mix white rice with purple mountain
rice harvested from the Cordilleras, and these white grains would soak
up the rich purple color of the mountain grains as they simmered together in our rice cooker. Though an adventurous cook, he refused to
use ingredients he deemed "disgusting" or "uncivilized," such as brain,
entrails, or feet. We had urbanidad, as some would say, but we did not
turn up our noses at local ingredients or native delicacies sold on the
street such as suman, a rice cake wrapped in banana or palm leaf, or
tinudok, deep-fried glutinous rice balls. My father had made sure that
we ate well, and ate healthy, and he knew that one could find good food
in the unlikeliest of places.

"How could these people whom I entrusted you with do this to you?"
my father remarked after giving me a hug. I had to leave home to realize
that while other adults could be indifferent to my suffering, my parents
could feel in their bodies the hunger and pain that my own body felt.

My parents saw to it that they fed me well whenever I visited them
in Baguio, or whenever they came to visit me at the UP Diliman campus. At UP, they took me to fancy restaurants like Chocolate Kiss or the

much humbler Rodic's at the UP Shopping Center (where I had the best caldereta of my life), but in my dorm room I dreamed of coming home to Baguio, which would always be my home because the food was familiar and nourishing. In our home, pansit (noodles) was a regular offering and not just a meal prepared on special occasions. If one ran out of ideas for dinner, one could always make pansit. Vegetables, protein, carbohydrates—pansit combines all these essential components of a meal, bringing together a variety of flavors in a single dish. Unlike the pansit served at turu-turos that's drenched in cooking oil and soy sauce and flavored with pork fat, my father's pansit was light but flavorful, seasoned with leftover adobo and shrimp. I don't remember ever visiting Baguio during my university years without having my father's pansit—his reasoning was I could easily pack the leftovers in a Tupperware container that I could bring with me when I returned to Manila. The dish filled the stomach while packing a punch of flavors.

As fate took me farther away from my home, first to Los Baños for my first teaching job, then to Austin, Texas, for my MFA, and then to Wellington, New Zealand, for doctoral studies, pansit became a special offering that my father prepared whenever I visited my parents in Baguio. Whenever I was home, my father asked me to sit with him in the kitchen as he chopped vegetables, deveined shrimp, shredded leftover adobo, and talked about his writing. He often reassured me that I didn't have to help him as he prepared this dish. "Just sit with me and talk," he said. "Tell me your stories." ◆

PANSIT BIHON GUISADO

STIR-FRIED RICE NOODLES WITH SHRIMP AND ADOBO

PREPARATION TIME: 1 hour

YIELD: 4 servings

2 dried mushrooms

1 ½ cups warm water

½ cup leftover chicken and/or pork adobo meat, shredded

1 tablespoon red or white wine (optional)

3 tablespoons vegetable oil, divided

4–6 cloves garlic, minced

1 small to medium onion, cut into slivers

1–2 celery ribs, chopped

1 small red bell pepper, seeded and cut into thin strips

¼ cup fresh shrimp, peeled and deveined, or dried shrimp

¼ cup soy sauce, plus a dash for serving

1 medium carrot, cut into thin strips

1 chayote or zucchini, cut into thin strips, or ½ head broccoli or napa cabbage, chopped

½ pound bihon (dry rice noodles) (see Note on page 154)

½ teaspoon freshly ground black pepper

Dash freshly squeezed calamansi juice, for serving (optional)

Soak the mushrooms in the warm water for at least 20 minutes. Drain the mushrooms, reserve the soaking liquid, and thinly slice the mushrooms. Combine the adobo and wine (if using) in a bowl.

Heat 2 tablespoons of the oil in a large skillet or wok over medium heat until it shimmers. Add the garlic and stir-fry until light gold. Add the onion and cook, stirring occasionally, for about 2 minutes, or until translucent. Stir in the celery and bell pepper. Cook, stirring occasionally, for 2 minutes. Add the adobo. If you are using fresh shrimp, add them, too. Cook, stirring, for about 1 minute. Remove from the heat and set aside.

The word pansit *comes from the Hokkien word* pien sit, pien *meaning "finished" or, more accurately, "cooked food." It was originally a Chinese merchant's meal meant to ease homesickness. It became a popular takeout food during Spanish colonial times among women working in cigar factories, and was prepared and sold by* pansiteros *who later set up shop in* pansiterias *that served Chinese food to workers and the traveling public. Pansit bihon, which uses a clear rice noodle, and pansit canton, which uses a thicker egg noodle, are regular offerings at fiestas. Pansit has come to symbolize long life and health in Filipino culture, and is commonly served at birthdays, baptisms, and New Year's celebrations.*

Recipe continues >

Pour the reserved mushroom soaking liquid into a saucepan and add the soy sauce, mushrooms, carrot, and chayote. If you are using dried shrimp, add those, too. Bring the mixture to a boil over high heat. Add the noodles and toss with the rest of the ingredients. As the noodles become tender, separate them until they are able to mix evenly with the veggies, about 3 minutes.

When the noodles have completely absorbed the liquid and are chewable, stir in the celery, bell pepper, and adobo mixture. Season with the black pepper and mix thoroughly. Pour in the remaining 1 tablespoon oil. Reduce the heat to low to gently fry the noodles for about 2 minutes. Serve with an extra dash of soy sauce and calamansi juice, if using.

NOTE: If your package of rice noodles recommends presoaking the dry noodles, do so and then reduce the mushroom soaking water from 1½ cups to ½ cup.

EVERY SUNSET

I N OUR APARTMENT in Toronto, I gaze out on the city skyline framed by slate-gray skies, thinking of how much I've grown. When I came to Canada with my family, I started a new life with zero dollars to my name. After years of work in hotels, overnight shifts for celebrities who partied until dawn, gallons of midnight oil burned to finish my college degree, and a challenging internship at a national magazine, I finally could afford a place of my own in this corner of the world. A place where I could relax and unwind—a place I would love to become my home.

Today, like many other days, I long for food from my homeland, the Philippines. But this time, I pine for something a bit out of the ordinary: a rice noodle dish with shrimp sauce called pansit palabok. This is my special-occasion dish—a must-have on my birthdays. Although it isn't my birthday, my partner, Iain, knows that once I have a craving for Filipino food, there's no stopping me until that craving is gratified. Even if he has plans to make beer (he's an avid home brewer) or a big pot of beans (his favorite pantry staple), he gladly hands over the reins of the kitchen to me.

I hardly cooked until I moved out of my parents' house in Canada. In the Philippines, I and most kids I knew had a nanny or relative who did most of the cooking. But I knew that my ideal self—a financially independent, socially conscious, bike-riding millennial—would not be complete without learning how to cook pansit palabok and many of the other Filipino foods I love.

Pansit palabok brings to mind my 18th birthday. I attended a hotel school in Manila at that time, and while most of my college friends

NASTASHA ALLI works as a software support consultant in Toronto and loves living in a town where fantastic food and drink experiences are never far away. She's hooked on books about culinary history and writes about Philippine foodways. She is the creator of the podcast *Exploring Filipino Kitchens*, where she talks about Filipino food, history, culture, and travel.

trained to be chefs in cruise ships and high-end restaurants, I prepared to work for luxury hotels. After class, to celebrate my entrance into legal adulthood, my friends and I headed to a joint along Manila Bay, the kind that served pulutan (food accompaniments to beverages), with buckets of ice-cold beer on sometimes rickety plastic tables that spilled onto the sidewalk. The incoming breeze always felt sticky and smelled of exhaust fumes, cigarette smoke, and salty sea air. Of course, we ordered pansit palabok, a large platter of it. It came in a mound on a round, woven, banana leaf–lined tray called a bilao. The rice noodles, white as a blank canvas, were smothered with a rich sauce as blazing orange as the setting sun on Manila Bay. A generous scattering of sliced boiled eggs, crunchy chicharron, tinapa (smoked fish), shrimp, squid, and scallions adorned the sauce. We clinked beer bottles and took photos of our tipsy selves (before selfies were even a thing). It was my duty to portion it out: noodles that tended to clump together, palabok sauce notorious for its chunky consistency, and toppings that were almost impossible to evenly distribute to everyone.

That dinner felt like home to me as a teenager in Manila. I was surrounded by friends and the comfort of familiarity. But the memory also carried a sense of excitement for the mysterious future; none of us knew then to which corner of the world life would take us.

What gives palabok sauce that sunny orange color? I wonder. I swing by one of the two bedrooms of our Toronto apartment to browse through my library—a shelf packed with Filipino cookbooks. I pull five books from the shelf, look up five different recipes for the dish, and find the unanimous answer to my question: annatto seeds! Luckily, annatto seeds are available at Latino grocery stores in Toronto. While I flip through the pages, I think about how I can adapt the ingredients and cooking techniques used in the Philippines to my North American kitchen. Whole shrimp, for example, requires a trip to an Asian grocery store, but is absolutely necessary to bring out the depth of flavor that can only be extracted from crushed shrimp heads. Understanding that the shrimp flavor needs time to break down and mingle with other ingredients taught me to be patient in building the tasty sauce that is distinct to palabok.

When I cook, there's one thing I must contend with: the size of my kitchen. In the kitchen, Iain and I rock to early records of The Doors playing as loud as we want, as long as we don't move much. Space constraints often go hand in hand with living in a big city. In fact, it takes no more than two seconds to cross our kitchen: look right and everything on our ceiling-height IKEA shelves is within reach; bend slightly to load dirty dishes into the portable dishwasher stowed in a corner; turn right to heat up the burner and oven; swivel left for the cutting and prep board; take another step to stand in front of the sink.

Iain talks about how learning *mise en place,* a French culinary term for "putting everything in its place," was a turning point in his success with cooking. He says, "Measuring and organizing all your ingredients before starting any part of the actual cooking process means a properly prepared dish, instead of a burnt sauce."

So, I lay out my ingredients: peeled shrimp and squid rings drain in a colander; shrimp heads, shells, and tails for the broth sit in a bowl; chopped pork belly is piled on a plate; minced garlic, shallots, and scallions await on a chopping board; eggs are covered with water in a pot ready to be boiled; noodles soak in a large bowl; a strainer and a whisk are within grabbing distance. I'm ready to cook.

As I wait for the shrimp stock to boil, a comforting feeling surrounds me like a warm hug—everything's in its place. I take a deep breath to savor the moment. This new place delivers experiences I could only dream about when I was 18.

As I wait for the shrimp stock to boil, a comforting feeling surrounds me like a warm hug—everything's in its place. I take a deep breath to savor the moment. This new place delivers experiences I could only dream about when I was 18. Me with a half-sleeve tattoo and my bearded partner, preparing my favorite dish together, while snow the color of rice noodles falls outside the window and city lights blur in the distance moments after the setting sun turns the horizon into another vivid orange hue.

Cooking palabok from scratch in Canada, like making a home thousands of miles away from my original home, is not without challenges. It's an undertaking that requires time, effort, and understanding. And through the bumps and the hurdles, I persist to prepare this dish so closely connected to feelings of being home, of being around people who make me happy. Cooking lets us share experiences with others in intimate ways.

Dinner is served. Iain and I clink bottles of his homemade beer. I'm overwhelmed with a feeling of satisfaction not just from how briny and savory each forkful of pansit tastes, but because palabok is, like many great dishes, made with a lot of love. Though it's just me and Iain sitting down to a platter of homemade pansit palabok this time, it feels every bit as homey and as hopeful as my 18th birthday dinner. ◆

PANSIT PALABOK

RICE NOODLES WITH SEAFOOD AND THICK SHRIMP SAUCE

PREPARATION TIME: 2 hours

YIELD: 3–4 servings

Palabok *is a term Tagalog people have given this dish. Across different cookbooks, however, the basic recipe for rice noodles coated with shrimp sauce and toppings is called* pansit luglug. *In his book* Cocina Sulipeña *on Pampanga cooking, Chef Gene Gonzalez explains that* luglug *means "to dunk or rinse in liquid," referring to noodles dipped in stock then draped with a heavy sauce. Regional variations such as* pansit malabon *are essentially* pansit luglug, *enriched with locally abundant seafood.*

PORK STOCK

½ pound pork belly, sliced across the grain into ½-inch-thick strips

½ teaspoon coarse sea salt

1 bay leaf

½ teaspoon fish sauce

4 cups water

SHRIMP STOCK

2 tablespoons annatto seeds

1 cup hot water

1 pound whole shrimp (thawed if frozen), heads, shells, and tails removed and reserved

1 bay leaf

EGGS AND SQUID

1 tablespoon vegetable oil

4 large eggs

½ pound squid, cut into rings

PALABOK SAUCE

4 cloves garlic, minced

1 large shallot, minced

2 tablespoons cornstarch

ASSEMBLY

½ pound bihon (dry rice noodles), soaked in cold water

3 scallions (green parts only), sliced

½ cup crumbled chicharron (pork rind; optional)

4 calamansi, halved, or 1 lime, cut into wedges (optional)

Make the pork stock: Combine the pork belly, salt, bay leaf, fish sauce, and water in a medium saucepan. Bring to a boil over high heat. Reduce the heat to low and simmer the stock for 20 minutes. Using a strainer, remove the pork belly and transfer to a plate. Discard the bay leaf. Keep the stock at a low simmer until the other components are ready.

Recipe continues >

Make the shrimp stock: Steep the annatto seeds in the hot water for 20 minutes. Strain the liquid into a medium saucepan and discard the annatto seeds. Add the shrimp heads, shells, and tails and the bay leaf to the annatto water. Bring to a boil over medium heat. Remove the pot from the heat and let the shrimp stock rest for 15 minutes. Strain the stock into a large bowl and discard the solids. Remove and reserve ⅓ cup of the stock in a separate bowl.

Make the eggs and squid: Heat the vegetable oil in a saucepan over medium heat until it shimmers. Add the reserved pork belly pieces and fry until golden brown, about 20 minutes. Transfer to a plate lined with paper towels. Set aside. Leave 1 tablespoon of the rendered fat in the saucepan and discard the rest. Set the pan aside.

Put the eggs in a small pot and add enough water to cover them. Bring to a boil over medium heat, then immediately take the pot off the heat and cover it. Let the eggs sit, covered, in the water for 12 minutes. Then drain, peel, and slice the eggs. Set the egg slices aside.

Using a strainer, dunk the shrimp into the simmering pork stock and blanch for about 1 minute, or until the pieces turn pink. Drain the shrimp and set them aside. Repeat this blanching process with the squid rings, making sure to take them out after exactly 1 minute. Continue simmering the pork stock.

Make the palabok sauce: Place the saucepan with the rendered pork fat over medium heat. Add the garlic and shallot. Cook, stirring, for 3 to 5 minutes, until the shallot begins to caramelize. Whisk the cornstarch into the reserved ⅓ cup shrimp stock to use as a thickener. Pour the remaining bowl of shrimp stock into the saucepan. Slowly whisk in the cornstarch mixture. Continue whisking until the sauce thickens, about 5 minutes. Set the palabok sauce aside.

To assemble: Bring the pork stock to a boil. Drain the soaking water from the rice noodles, then add them to the pot. Cook for 3 to 4 minutes. Drain the noodles and set them aside. Discard the pork stock.

To serve, use tongs to portion the rice noodles onto plates. Ladle the palabok sauce over the noodles. Generously garnish each plate with the fried pork belly, shrimp, squid, eggs, scallions, chicharron, and calamansi, if using.

A PLAIN BOWL OF NOODLES

PAOLO ESPANOLA
is a former accoun-
tant and an ordinary
lover of food. Unable
to accept 16-hour
workdays staring at
Excel spreadsheets,
he started a food blog
as an act of rebellion
amid his elders' con-
cern that he "might
get deported" for not
throwing his all into
his day job. Paolo
now works at a social
media tech start-up
during the day; at
night, he produces
a podcast, dreams
up menus, and plans
pop-up dinners. He
believes—naively,
according to people
wiser than he—that
food can be used
to solve most of the
world's problems and
one day hopes he
can use food to help
others believe in their
potential, connect
with their roots, and
realize we can all be
breaking bread as one
race in this strange
world of ours.

T HERE WAS NO romance during my mealtimes. This isn't a story
of waddling onto a stool and helping my mother knead bread, nor
will this be a nostalgic remembrance of my lola (or ama in Hokkien),
who had stopped cooking her legendary Chinese pumpkin cakes many
years before I was born. Days blurred by in a complete and oppressive
boredom during my childhood years in Saudi Arabia means this won't
be a recounting of some strange and exotic Filipino dish I discovered
in some local's nipa hut. In fact, this will be a story as mundane and
unassuming as the dish it's inspired by.

I don't really recall the first time I tasted pansit molo. It may have
been just another night in our second-floor apartment in downtown
Al-Khobar, a crowded city filled with migrant workers and their cuisines that was a far cry from the barren deserts the media makes Saudi
Arabia out to be. Our table was adorned with a clear plastic cover for
easier cleaning, and the flower designs on our plates were faded and
cracked from decades of scraping every grain of rice after meals. My
mother didn't emerge from the kitchen, as you might imagine, amidst
the fragrant aroma of bagoong—a goddess floating on clouds of garlic. Instead, the petite Chinese woman came out hot, sweaty, and overworked from attempting to cook on a three-burner gas stovetop while
switching loads of laundry in the washing machine not two paces behind her. She was forbidden from cooking by traditionalist parents as a
child, and when she married my dad and told him this fact decades ago,
he simply stated that if she loved him, she would learn. He promptly
took a shower while my mother proceeded to deep-fry and burn raw

rice. At the time, my attempts to help a self-taught cook were confined to stirring the rice to make sure it didn't burn (because a rice cooker was out of the question) or snapping green beans in half (because using a knife on beans was inexplicably inappropriate), while she took a breather to record another episode of Martha Stewart.

Dinnertime was a Herculean effort for my parents to get my brother and me to stop doing whatever it was children could do in an urban jungle with few open places in which to play, and after the umpteenth call to the table, we sat down to plates of white rice, soup, fruits, and ulam. My dad, who grew up one of nine on a rural farm in Antique, Philippines, was proudly provinciano, or what Americans might call a bumpkin, and refused to entertain any meals that reeked of "non-Filipino-ness." Shepherd's pies were met with grumbles, fusilli con maiale with squinted eyes, and fried chicken, the epitome of perfection, required white rice and soup at the minimum. And so when pansit molo came to the table, with its plain white noodles, equally plain filling, and simple garnish of fried garlic and chopped scallions, my dad would check for the required accompaniment of white jasmine rice (not basmati, not Bomba, not brown) and ulam, nod his approval, and begin eating.

It wasn't that I disliked it per se, but my mother's pansit molo was a far cry from the versions I later tasted in the actual Molo district of Iloilo in the Philippines. It lacked the heartiness of a real stock (or at least one fortified with Magic Sarap and/or Aji-No-Moto seasoning) in favor of water flavored with salt; the chicken filling couldn't provide the same lip-smacking qualities of pork due to the latter being banned in the country; and many of the wrappers often broke, revealing the shriveled meat inside. So underwhelming was this particular soup that I could usually tell how busy my mom was with housekeeping duties based on our dinner. Sinigang with mixed meat chop suey? 'Twas a good day. Pansit molo and fried fish? Definitely overworked.

I could usually tell how busy my mom was with housekeeping duties based on our dinner. Sinigang with mixed meat chop suey? 'Twas a good day. Pansit molo and fried fish? Definitely overworked.

Even at Guakong's tiamlay (Grandfather's store) in Hokkien, the soup was an affair borne of necessity: eaten in the dark, cobweb-ridden back room with the sales ladies, or while standing in front of the cash register. I simply have no particularly fond memories of pansit molo. This extends to much of the food I ate as a child: Frankenstein creations made by mixing Filipino sentiments, Chinese techniques, and my mom's obsession with Martha Stewart's cooking show that left me full but definitely not as inspired as many of my food contemporaries' experiences, over which they wax poetic.

It wasn't until my interest in food exploded during college—for reasons still unclear to me, as my friends and family did their best to dissuade me from such a lowly, undignified, and unfit-for-a-Tsinoy-businessman-to-be profession—that I began to see the dishes of my past differently. The vegetable-laden laswas stood out in my memory when everyone else in Minnesota, where I attended college, saw Pinoy food confined to adobo, Spam, and garlic fried rice. Even adobo, for which my mom had three versions (pork-free original, Antiqueño, and Tsinoy), became a link to my mixed heritage that was the cause of much confusion in places where the slightest hint of an Arabic connection made you the butt of "terrorist jokes." Pansit molo, on the other hand, remained stubbornly plain and unadorned throughout the years. Even as my friends and I started hosting pop-up dinners in New York, catering parties, and writing and speaking about food, we made our own spins on everything from ensaladang talong to kinilaw, but not once did the soup reappear, not even in my own house.

At a particular dinner in an affluent Upper East Side apartment where we had to cook four courses, one from each of the Visayan regions, I was forced to reconsider this mixture of water, salt, noodles, and meat. The Internet offered no variations for me to play off of, and in the end, we did our best to create our own take on the dish that refused alteration: an umami-laced broth with dried shiitake mushrooms and Chinese herbs, with water chestnuts for crunch and garlic for flavor in the chicken filling, and . . . well, that was it. The diners' positive reactions to it prompted me to cook it for myself once more at home sans the herbs, water chestnuts, and flavorings (due to laziness, not lack of ingredients), and when I looked down at the broken dumplings, the thin salted water, and the blank stares of the pork and shrimp peering from under my chopsticks, I saw my mom's molo back from the grave of obscurity as plain as ever.

You may think there was some great philosophical insight to be had here, some pithy statement about the value of simplicity. So philosophizing for philosophy's sake, I suppose the pansit molo was an apt description of our days and a solid anchor in a city obsessed with the novel, the Instagrammable, the clickable, the brag-worthy. Behind each bowl of broth was a long line of Chinese traders who settled in Molo, stirring cauldrons of the soup. Each broken noodle mirrored by the many others caused by wrappers hurriedly wrapped by pansiteria owners in years long gone. And the plain filling representative of the comforting mundaneness in our days as the world changes in dizzying speeds around us. Sometimes, food is just food, and while dishes change over time (one variant I ended up making featured dumplings filled with pesto atop heirloom rice risotto rather than broth), they don't have to. We spend our days chasing all that glitters, wondering why we're not on the covers of our own magazines, forgetting that living under blue skies is cause for wonder and amazement already.

Philosophy aside, I was just one average kid in a nondescript second-floor apartment in Queens, sitting on a folded blanket atop a yoga mat with an apple crate for a table, slurping a bowl of plain noodles, filled with plain meat, swimming in plain broth, thinking plain thoughts. ◆

PANSIT MOLO

MEAT AND SHRIMP DUMPLING SOUP
WITH SHIITAKE MUSHROOMS

This isn't the only way to prepare pansit molo, and this recipe intentionally does not dictate how much seasoning one should use, the exact method of preparation, or the precise results. Cooking is a deeply personal thing and we should treat it as such. Want to use chicken instead of pork? Do it. Prefer to make your own stock? Go for it! Lucky and skilled enough to use heritage Kurobuta pork and handmade wrappers in a tomato consommé topped with calamansi foam? Awesome!

PREPARATION TIME: 1 hour
YIELD: 3–4 servings

4 cups vegetable broth or water

8 (or more) dried shiitake mushrooms

½ pound shrimp, peeled, deveined, and finely chopped (see Note on page 168)

½ pound ground pork, preferably 80:20 fat ratio

½ head garlic, minced

1 medium shallot, minced

1 handful fresh chives, finely chopped

½ (8-ounce) can water chestnuts, drained and finely chopped (optional)

1 large egg, lightly beaten

2 tablespoons kosher salt, soy sauce, fish sauce, or bagoong alamang, or to taste

1 (12-ounce) package wonton wrappers, thawed if frozen

1 package Chinese soup herb mix (see Note on page 168; optional)

Chopped scallions, for garnish

Soy sauce and calamansi (or other citrus) juice, for serving

Combine the vegetable broth and mushrooms in a saucepan. Bring the mixture to a simmer over medium-low heat. Reduce the heat to low, cover, and leave to simmer while you prepare the dumplings.

In a large bowl, combine the shrimp, pork, garlic, shallot, chives, water chestnuts (if using), and egg lightly by hand, taking care not to turn the mixture mushy. Add the salt. (You can use as much or as little salt as you want since you can set aside a small amount of it for dipping later, should your dumplings turn out too bland.)

Recipe continues >

Place a wonton wrapper on a clean work surface so that it looks like a diamond. Cover the rest of the wrappers with a damp cloth to keep them from drying out. Place about 1 teaspoon of the filling mixture in the center of the wonton wrapper. Fold the bottom corner up and over the mixture, covering it. Using fingers moistened in water, fold the left and right corners over to seal the dumpling. The result should be a dumpling with no meat showing and the top corner poking straight up like a nun's headdress. Repeat this process until you've used all the filling.

Stir the Chinese soup herbs, if using, into the simmering broth. Working in batches, add the dumplings to the broth, without crowding, and cook for 3 to 5 minutes, until they float. Check one by cutting it open. If the meat filling no longer looks raw, remove the dumplings with a slotted ladle and distribute into soup bowls. If the filling is not cooked through, simmer for another minute. Repeat this process with the remaining dumplings.

Taste and season the broth as needed. Remove and discard the Chinese herbs. Ladle the broth over the dumplings in the bowls. Distribute the shiitake in the bowls, garnish with chopped scallions, and serve with a few squirts of soy sauce and calamansi juice.

NOTE: If your shrimp have their shells and heads on, remove them and put them in with the mushrooms to add flavor to the broth. Before adding the dumplings to the broth, squeeze the liquid out of the shrimp heads and shells before removing and discarding them.

Packaged Chinese soup herb mixes containing ingredients such as wolfberry fruit, jujubes, and lovage rhizome are available at Asian groceries, usually in the spice/powdered soups/tea aisle, at traditional Chinese medicine shops, or online.

CHAPTER 6
RICE

E VERY FILIPINO DISH may have evolved or undergone alterations over the years, but one thing has stayed more or less constant: the rice that accompanies it. Good old steamed white rice is the essential and default canvas on which colorful and flavorful ulam are counterbalanced. It is eaten for lunch and dinner, and sometimes also for breakfast and in-between meals. Aside from its supporting role to ulam, rice serves other significant culinary functions in Philippine cooking. It's the main ingredient in stand-alone treats such as paella, arroz concoctions (such as arroz caldo and arroz valenciana), and a vast array of rice cakes. This chapter features dishes—both savory and sweet—in which rice plays the lead.

CAN'T HAVE ONE WITHOUT
THE OTHER

FOLLOWING BRITISH TRADITION, I was carted off halfway around
the world from my home in Hong Kong to boarding school in
the UK at the tender age of 13. When people ask how it was, I would
say that I loved everything about it, from the pseudo-independence of
being away from home to forming friendships that would last a lifetime.
But there was one thing that I wasn't particularly enamored with, and
that was the food—or, rather, my school's inability to cook rice for an
Asian palate. (Or in my words back then, "The British don't know how to
cook rice!") Little did I know that being in this situation would spark a
curiosity in me that would develop into a passion for food and cooking
later in life.

Being born in Hong Kong to a Filipina mother and a British father
meant growing up with a myriad of cuisines. Our mother did most of the
cooking in the kitchen, and dinners themselves would range from East
to West to strange mixes of foods we children liked—I remember chicken
nuggets and rice being a firm favorite, or pretty much anything and rice.
I was a rice-eating machine. Having such a varied menu at home meant
that the food we had access to while growing up wasn't necessarily dominated by Filipino food, which is probably why quite a lot of Filipino
dishes don't have that same nostalgic quality for me as they do for others.

However, one thing that I do remember and feel nostalgic about is
my mother's adobo. It was one of my favorite dishes of hers. The smell
was instantly recognizable: that savory-sour mixture of soy and vinegar,
slowly winding its way through the house, beckoning me to the kitchen
once the scent hit my nose. Back then, I wasn't fond of eating meat off

MIKE CORBYN moved to Tokyo from London and is the cofounder of The Adobros, a supper club he owns with his adobo-loving brother, Mark. Mike's passion for great food stems from growing up surrounded by a veritable smorgasbord of Southeast Asian cuisines, with the chance to try something new at every corner. He believes that some of the best memories are made over the dinner table and that good food brings people together, whether they realize it or not. It is an atmosphere that he strives to replicate in each dinner that The Adobros host.

the bone (I could be a picky child at times), so after I tore off whatever meat I felt like eating, it was on to the main course: rice and adobo sauce—or, should I say, adobo sauce with a bit of rice. I remember I would pour it extremely liberally over my rice, drinking it like soup after every other spoonful from the serving dish to my plate. I was addicted.

I helped my mother from time to time in the kitchen, but my interest in cooking didn't develop for several years. I always say that my first foray into cooking was out of necessity and personal survival more than anything else.

At the boarding school, one thing I made note of early on was that those in Year 11 (15 to 16 years old) and above were allowed access to the small kitchens in each of the boardinghouses. Granted, they mainly used the kitchen to make toast, because who at that age knew how to cook?

With this in mind, the summer before my entry into Year 11, I begged my mother to show me how to cook "good" rice. I am forever grateful for her response, which was to tell me that if I wanted to learn how to cook rice, I should also learn how to cook something to eat with the rice—specifically how to cook her adobo. Unknown to me at the time, my mother was instilling in me the tradition of ulam, the very Filipino idea of having a main dish specifically to go with rice. I thought to myself, *My mother is a genius!*

And with that I set out to arm myself with the skills needed to satisfy my cravings for rice when in the UK. I was surprised to learn that my mother didn't have a standard recipe for her adobo, and when I asked her how she made it, she told me matter-of-factly, "Taste is everything; you need to make sure you keep tasting it as the sauce develops and adjust as necessary. A good cook will know how to make their food based on taste."

My mother also told me that everyone's adobo was different and that eventually my own adobo would evolve. That turned out to be true; over the years I have altered, adjusted, and tweaked my recipe, making it very much my own.

When the first term of Year 11 in boarding school began, I readied myself for my first time in the kitchen after a couple of months of practice at home. I went out on a weekend and bought all the ingredients. Plastic shopping bag in hand, I lurched to the kitchen nervous with excitement—I was going to cook a dish that I had been craving all week. My bare-bones workplace was a small kitchen typical of student houses: linoleum floors, cheap fittings, a suspicious-looking gas stovetop, and pots and pans that looked older than me.

The average schoolmate, if wanting a little more than toast, may have on a very rare occasion overcooked some pasta and slathered it in bottled tomato sauce (the Tesco Everyday Value brand being a top choice). But someone actually using the kitchen and taking up counter space for chopping garlic and portioning chicken was somewhat of a novelty. The initial jokes from passersby slowly turned into people popping their heads in and asking with genuine curiosity what on earth I was cooking. I was creating a smell they had never experienced before. They were intrigued and hooked by the smell of adobo.

This was where another pearl of wisdom from my mother came in: "Always make lots of food. Other people will always want some, and if they don't you can have lots of leftovers; after all, we know that adobo ages well." I had made plenty of food, so I offered a taste to anyone who wanted some. Their satisfaction and appreciation of my food laid the foundation for, years down the line, gatherings where I would cook large meals for friends. Cooking for one isn't as much fun.

Filipinos are probably one of the most rice-obsessed people I know, and no meal is complete without that mound of steaming, fluffy, fragrant rice. Rice to me is the ultimate comfort, the constant at every meal. Ulam and rice exist with each other in perfect balance, one not complete without the other. While the ulam can change, rice grounds the meal and brings everything together. Rice is home. ◆

ARANDOBO BALLS

DEEP-FRIED CHICKEN ADOBO—STUFFED RICE BALLS

This dish is similar to Italian arancini, which are deep-fried rice balls that are usually stuffed with a meat sauce and cheese. This version uses adobo. Any adobo can be used for this recipe, but I've found that an adobo made with bony chicken legs provides a high enough collagen content to gelatinize the sauce when chilled.

TOTAL TIME: 2½ hours
YIELD: 16–20 balls

2 tablespoons vegetable oil, plus more for deep-frying

1 head garlic, minced

1¾ pounds bone-in, skin-on chicken thighs and drumsticks

2½ cups cane vinegar or rice vinegar

1¾ cups light soy sauce

2–3 bay leaves

Freshly ground black pepper, to taste

1 cup low-sodium chicken broth

Cornstarch, for thickening

2 cups cooked short-grain or sushi rice

2 medium eggs

1 cup panko breadcrumbs

Salt, to taste

Heat the oil in a large pot over medium heat. Add the garlic and cook, stirring occasionally, until fragrant, about 1 minute. Add the chicken. Stir with the garlic for 1 minute and then add the vinegar, soy sauce, and bay leaves. Season with pepper.

Add the chicken broth, plus enough water to ensure that the chicken pieces are completely submerged in liquid. Bring the mixture to a boil, then reduce the heat to low and simmer for about 1 hour, or until the chicken is cooked and falling off the bone. Be sure to taste the adobo along the way and adjust the soy sauce, vinegar, or chicken broth (or water if you've run out) as needed.

Transfer the chicken to a plate and raise the heat to medium. Continue to cook the sauce for about 1 minute, or until it is thick enough to coat the back of a spoon. Make a cornstarch slurry by mixing equal parts cornstarch and cold water in a bowl. Stir it in, 1 tablespoon at a time, until the sauce is as thick as gravy.

Recipe continues >

Reserve ¼ cup of the sauce for reheating later on. Cool the rest of the sauce as quickly as possible by filling a roasting pan with ice, placing another pan on top, and pouring the sauce into the top pan. The sauce should start to gel as it cools down.

While you're waiting for the sauce to cool, pull the chicken meat from the skin and bones and shred the meat. Discard the bones but reserve the skin—you can blast it in the oven until crispy for a delicious snack or as an accompaniment to the arandobo balls.

Scoop about 1 tablespoon of the rice into one hand and flatten it in your palm to form a circle. Add about 1 teaspoon of the shredded chicken to the center, followed by a teaspoon of the jellied adobo sauce. Wrap the rice around the chicken and add more as necessary to fill any gaps. Set the rice ball aside. Repeat this process until either the rice or chicken runs out.

Make an egg wash by beating the eggs in a bowl. Pour the panko crumbs into a separate bowl. One by one, dip the rice balls into the egg wash and then into the panko, coating them evenly.

Transfer the reserved and remaining (if any) adobo sauce to a small sauce-pan and heat over low heat; keep warm while you deep-fry the arandobo balls.

Pour about 2 inches of vegetable oil into a large pot. Heat the oil over medium-high heat until a deep-fry thermometer registers 375°F. Working in batches so as not to overcrowd the pan, drop the balls in and fry until golden, about 3 minutes. Transfer the balls to a wire rack and season with salt. Repeat with the remaining balls.

Serve with the warmed adobo sauce.

NOTE: After you bread the rice balls, you can freeze them for frying later. Just place them in a single layer on a baking sheet lined with plastic wrap. Cover with plastic wrap and freeze. Once frozen, you can transfer them to zip-top bags and return to the freezer. They will keep for at least a month. Thaw before deep-frying.

MY PLATE IS FULL

{AS TOLD TO THE EDITOR}

ROSING ARGENTARA, our maid for 19 years, couldn't look me in the eye when she asked if she could speak with me. There was something about her manner and tone of voice that clasped my heart. I had a feeling that the moment I had been dreading was about to come.

It was 1970 in Boston, Massachusetts—months after man's first step on the moon but long before dishwashers and microwave ovens were common in households. Foodwise, flaming fondues, junk food, and Howard Johnson's were on trend.

Aside from a career in dietetics at Boston City Hospital and work as a political, cultural, and humanitarian activist, I was also a mother of four (ages five, three, two, and one) and expecting a fifth. The involvement in family life of my husband, Tony, a cardiothoracic surgical resident, could best be described as "hit-and-run." To say the least, Rosing was my trusted helper and friend. Without her I had no idea how I would manage.

Rosing was the firstborn child of a big family in Gabu, a barrio along the pristine beaches of the South China Sea in Ilocos Norte, Philippines. Her mother had approached mine to ask if we could employ her daughter as a maid. Their family had been in dire need of financial help, and though we already had maids, Mother couldn't refuse. I could still remember the first time I saw Rosing: 16 years old and as puny as a fifth grader.

I, 11 at that time, had whined, "I don't want Rosing to be our maid! I want her to be my playmate!"

She worked for us, nevertheless, and bunked in a room with two other housemaids and the cook in our stately home in Ilocos Norte, headed by my father, Justice Santiago R. Ranada. Papang, my father, belonged to one of the early Ilustrado (native-born intellectual) families in the region. His

MARILYN RANADA DONATO moved to the United States in 1962 for postgraduate training in dietetics and has lived there ever since. She has worked at hospitals in Michigan, Massachusetts, and Virginia and as an independent private practitioner, nutrition lecturer, and food editor for several Philippine American newspapers. In 1992, she received the Americanism Medal from the Daughters of the American Revolution General James Breckinridge chapter and the Women of Distinction award. Marilyn is the author of the cookbook *Philippine Cooking in America*.

clan made a fortune plying the China Sea and Pacific Ocean with fishing vessels manned by sea captains and fishermen. The assortment of fresh seafood they caught—fish large and small, shrimp of all sizes, lobster, squid, octopus, and clams—were sold wholesale. A portion of their best catch was brought home for our family's consumption. This kindled my love for seafood, especially for paella, a free-style one-pot meal uniting different food groups in one dish: rice, seafood, meat, and vegetables.

Even though we had a live-in cook and maids like Rosing at our beck and call, Papang, a busy lawyer, sometimes found time to cook. Papang began his preparation by laying out the equipment he needed on the kitchen table: a heavy iron kawali, a wok-like pan; a kawa, a metal cauldron; and burnay, earthen jars. He then lined up the ingredients for inspection, making sure they were fresh and of the finest quality. When he took charge of cooking, the help made themselves scarce in the kitchen unless they were called in.

"Carmen, where's the mortar and pestle?" or "Carmen, sort the rice!" he roared, and Nana Carmen, our cook, scuttled in to do as she was told and scuttled back out as soon as her task was done.

Likewise, when we ate our meals, our domestic helpers stood by to wait on us. None joined us at the table. There had been a tacit but pronounced masters-and-servants divide; employer and employees, unlike the ingredients of paella, didn't mix.

Rosing, now 35, had met a nice Filipino man who lived in San Pedro, California. I knew it was just a matter of time before she followed her heart and left us. But still, I wasn't ready to receive this kind of news. Not yet. Not now.

Rosing had moved in with us five years before. I was relieved and overjoyed when my parents announced over the phone that I had a present on its way. We lived in New Haven, Connecticut, at that time and I was pregnant with our first child. Lo and behold, my mother's present was my favorite maid—Rosing, all four feet eleven inches and 90 pounds of her in the flesh, flown in all the way from the Philippines!

There was some hullabaloo during mealtime when Rosing first arrived. Notwithstanding our pleas, she refused to sit and eat with us at the table and instead carried on with the practice of segregation she was used to in the Philippines. Fed up, I put my foot down and said, "Rosing, we are in the United States! *You eat with us.*" Without a word, she fetched herself a plate and cutlery, pulled up a chair, and joined us for dinner. She had been a bona fide member of the family since then.

The moment I was dreading had come. Rosing asked for my blessing to leave so she could marry and raise a family of her own with the man she loved in San Pedro. Good for her! But what about me? My family? My life? How could she not have thought about us? I knew I would miss her immensely. I could have ordered her to stay, at least until I found someone to replace her or until I had everything under control (which, I realized, might not happen until my children turned into adults). I knew she'd stay if I told her to, but that would be selfish. The Golden Rule I lived by, drilled into my very being by my Catholic upbringing, nagged at my conscience. I couldn't stand in her way to happiness. I let her go.

Weeks later, I was back at our grand ancestral house in Ilocos Norte for a visit or, perhaps I should say, a retreat. The house looked more imposing than I recalled. The large capiz-shell sliding windows at the comedor, or dining room, were pushed apart, aiding the overhead mahogany-toned fan in turning the heat down in the room. The shiny hardwood floor overwhelmed: a dazzling reminder of the hours spent by the maid waxing it on hands and knees, followed by a vigorous leg scrub with a bunot, or coconut husk.

Papang and I sat at the long, 18-seat narrawood dining table. At the head of the table, on a brocade-upholstered chair with an intricately carved back, Papang looked imperial, an emperor on his throne.

"Marilyn, you are not going back to the United States! Not unless you take a maid with you!" he declared.

I half expected to hear a gavel pound the table. I accepted my sentence. Without a word, I rose and walked slowly back to my room. It felt like I was five, instead of a mother of four, soon to be five, children.

Miracle of miracles, we found a new maid, Virginia Escobar. Work on her passport and visa was rushed, and Virginia accompanied me back to Boston before my fifth child was born.

It's 1985 in Roanoke, Virginia. Months after man's first solo transatlantic flight in a helium balloon but years before the birth of the Internet and online recipes. Yuppies, with the help of Nancy Reagan, had brought cocktail parties with all their glitz and glamour back into vogue.

Contentious and radical assertions float around about food: you should eat protein separately from starch, include only one type of protein per meal, and eat fruit in isolation. Segregated eating is part of a campaign promising weight loss without portion-size restrictions and a lifestyle that keeps you fit and slim forever. These claims resonate to a population that is increasingly becoming health and figure conscious.

As a dietician, I compare good nutrition to the way we dress daily—underwear, skirt or trousers, top, socks or stockings, footwear, coat or jacket, etc.—each piece of clothing is part of an ensemble that meets a specific need, a desired way of life.

Aside from my private practice as a registered dietician, having finished a term as president of the board of directors of a Catholic organization, and having just released the fourth edition of a cookbook I wrote and published, I am a mother of six (yes, I had another one) and am 100 percent maidless. Virginia, like Rosing, met and married a nice man and left us two years before.

I am now the official and only cook of our family. I can whip up a mean paella—no sweat—with the help of my cookbook, the recipes of which Virginia helped me test.

I love paella because it is a harmonious blend of diversity: the mingling of produce from land and sea, the union of ingredients from varying food groups, and the interplay of an assortment of colors, flavors, shapes, and sizes. It's what makes each mouthful an exciting experience—a scrumptious symphony of aroma, textures, and tastes. Dividing food by class, such as eating just carbs at one meal then just protein at the next—never together—cannot be a step forward.

Yes, my two maids no longer work for us. But they remain a part of our lives. Once and again, Rosing, Virginia, and their families come together with mine. We gather at the table enjoying platefuls of mixed and all-inclusive Filipino paella. ◆

MEAT, SEAFOOD, AND VEGETABLE PAELLA

This recipe is adapted from the paella recipe that appears in my cookbook, Philippine Cooking in America, *which first hit the market in 1972. The idea to write and publish a cookbook came about in 1963, when a Chinese shop owner in Connecticut suggested that I write a Philippine cookbook because there weren't any around. While paella is typically considered comida española, this Filipinized version uses the more affordable tomato paste instead of saffron to color the dish and doesn't discriminate against the use of any type of rice.*

PREPARATION TIME: 1 hour

YIELD: 10–12 servings

5 cups water

2 teaspoons coarse sea salt, divided

12–15 mussels or fresh clams in shell

1½ pounds bone-in, skinless chicken thighs or breasts, cut into 2-inch pieces

1 pound boneless pork, cut into 1½-inch cubes

½ cup vegetable oil

4 cloves garlic, minced

1 medium onion, finely sliced

1 pound large shrimp, peeled and deveined

1 (6-ounce) can tomato paste

2 cups uncooked rice

Salt and freshly ground black pepper, to taste

1 cup frozen green peas, microwaved for 3 minutes

¼ cup sliced pimento

3 blue crabs in shell, boiled and halved (optional)

In a large stockpot, bring the water and 1 teaspoon of the salt to a boil over medium-high heat. Add the mussels. Bring the mixture back to a boil and then remove it from the heat. Transfer the mussels to a plate and set it aside. Pour the broth into a separate container and reserve.

Wash and pat dry the chicken and pork and season the meat with the remaining 1 teaspoon of salt. Heat the oil in the same pot over medium-high heat, add the meat, and fry until golden on all sides, 5 to 10 minutes. Transfer the meat to a plate and set aside.

Add the garlic and onion to the hot oil and cook, stirring occasionally, until the onion is semi-translucent, about 2 minutes. Add the shrimp and the fried chicken and pork. Cook, stirring occasionally, for 2 minutes. Add the tomato paste and rice. Stir and cook for about 3 minutes. Add the seafood broth. Cover and let boil rapidly for 1 minute. Stir once, cover again, reduce the heat to low, and simmer until the mixture is almost dry and the rice is almost cooked. Season with salt and pepper.

Carefully stir in the peas, pimento, and mussels. Arrange the crabs, if using, on top. Cover and continue cooking over low heat until the rice is fully cooked (high heat will cause the rice to burn). Serve right away.

THAT WHICH WE CALL CHAMPORADO

WHY ARE WE DOING THIS? I ask myself, a few minutes into the conversation I'm having with Mother. I begin pacing back and forth in my tiny living room from one end of my faux oriental rug to the other. I usually question the indirect exchanges my mother and I have over the phone. It's like we're two old people who are hard of hearing and trying to make conversation, or two people with so much to say that we don't have time to listen to each other, so we speak simultaneously without pause.

It's a lot of misunderstandings and unanswered questions, but I suppose there's some level of joy in creating that process together with her.

"Oh, it's probably spaghetti. You love spaghetti."

"Huh?"

"I packed that in your lunch all the time."

"I don't think I had spaghetti, Mother. Besides, this is about Filipino food. Name some of the dishes I had growing up that I may have forgotten."

"I used the Ragu. It's really easy to make. You loved it!" she reaffirmed.

Why are we doing this . . . and did she just say "*the* Ragu"?

"I can assure you I never had any spaghetti in my brown bag lunch, Mother. What about champorado? You made that for me before," which comes off as more of a question than a declaration.

"Oh, yeah, I did! And that's an easy one, too!" she finally agrees.

Her response recalls a memory, which is ultimately the purpose of the phone call.

RAY ESPIRITU is the proprietor of Isla Pilipina, an award-winning Filipino restaurant in Chicago. He and the team at Isla have been recognized by many local and national publications for their work, and they take pride in their commitment to reinventing themselves while delivering and expanding on a philosophy based on culture, family, and art. Outside of the restaurant, Ray is a visual artist and educator in the fields of creative philosophy and neo-esotericism.

Suddenly, it's like I was 11 again in our bungalow in Chicago. I'd been sitting at our kitchen table, the psychedelic vinyl tablecloth stuck to my forearms, the four chairs huddled close to each other because my parents decided to push one side of the table against the wall. Dad was playing Fleetwood Mac's *Rumours* album on full blast from the living room—at a time when Nine Inch Nails had just released *The Downward Spiral.*

There was leftover food out on the table from earlier in the day. And I remember the flies. There were always flies. We protected our precious leftovers from said flies with little tents—the type made of some kind of mesh, so you could still see the food through them. We had several of these tents in different colors and sizes sprawled across the table. They made the kitchen table look like a small Olympic village with a series of arenas, but instead of athletes and fans, it was fried rice or Spam inside them. Exciting nonetheless.

One thing that never made it into one of the domes was the champorado. It wasn't often that Mother made the dish, but when she did, it was a treat. Since the age of 11, I had an existential "why?" moment as to how simple the dish is to make. It's chocolate, it's rice, it has the world's supply of sugar embedded in it. And it's wonderful. This is the kind of dish that adheres to the lifestyle of a "simple man," which my colleagues have asserted I very much am.

The ritual was simple but meticulously crafted. Mother would first announce that she was going to make champorado. This gave my sister and me the opportunity to discuss how pleased we were with the selection and allowed us to renew some strength in our relationship with our mother, check our sugar inventory, reestablish faith in God, and so on.

The next phase of the ritual was during the cooking process. The chocolaty rice aroma slowly filled the room, engaging with any negative ions and allowing every aspect of our physical bodies to prepare for the magic about to take place. Lastly, the champorado was served, and the sun shone just that much brighter for the rest of the day.

Now, this magic I speak of is not the kind that creates a turning point in one's life. It's not the kind of dish that triggers a progressive movement of consciousness that sparks revolution. Champorado is just the kind of dish that makes you fold your hands and acknowledge, "Today, indeed, is a good day."

Before getting off the phone with my mother that evening, we somehow manage to talk a bit about champorado's easy preparation, obvious aesthetic (chocolate-colored rice), and narrow range of flavors. But mostly, we talk about the joy we shared together on many mornings, about how I did so poorly in elementary intramural basketball, the new ways to justify my parents having to work two jobs each, the discomfort of living in a crime-ridden neighborhood at the time, my sister's steadfast commitment to mastering Kenny G's "Forever in Love" on the piano, and most of all, we talk about how funny it all was because in a unique way, all those moments were immortalized through a safe space, which was our kitchen table, and oftentimes over a bowl of champorado.

It becomes clear to me that the candid and beautiful memories of my past are symbolized by this simple dish. And champorado is, indeed, the question "Why are we doing this?" in the form of food, the answer to which is found in the experience of it. Maybe the symbolism is a bit of a reach, but its simplicity in preparation and taste serves as a reminder to adhere to what is true, which is "now," and sometimes all the pain and pleasure of every moment is not as complex as we imagine them to be. Champorado is not and probably will never be a life-changing experience, but (speaking only for myself) it will forever be the kind of dish that will set the tone for, or recall, a pretty good day. ◆

CHAMPORADO

SWEET CHOCOLATE PORRIDGE

PREPARATION TIME: 20 minutes

YIELD: 3 servings

½ cup cocoa powder

3½ cups warm water, divided

1 cup sweet rice

½ cup granulated sugar

Evaporated milk or creamer, to taste, for serving

Champorado is the Filipino version of the Mexican champurrado, which is a thick chocolate-based drink. Chocolate and sugar remain the common denominators between the two. Although cocoa tablets are traditionally used for champorado, this recipe utilizes a more accessible replacement: cocoa powder. Much stirring is involved, but it'll keep you engaged in the process, which is a precious quality.

Dissolve the cocoa powder in 1 cup of the warm water. Set aside.

In a medium saucepan, combine the rice and remaining 2½ cups water. Bring to a boil over medium-high heat. Reduce the heat to low and cook, stirring constantly, for 30 seconds.

Pour the cocoa powder mixture into the saucepan of simmering rice. Continue cooking and stirring for about 10 minutes. Add the sugar and stir for another 5 minutes.

Serve in bowls and drizzle with evaporated milk.

Champorado (page 187)

Ginataang Bilo-Bilo (page 193)

SUMMER OF '92

O UR HAPPY DAYS were about to end. It was 1992, and I was 10. Kids crowded the arcades, challenged each other on *Street Fighter II*. Boyz II Men ruled the airwaves. Baggy jeans, worn as low as they'd go without falling off, were so popular they were a movement.

Reality struck my older brother, Alistair, and me. Our summer holidays were finished. The Nintendo we squabbled over, the Game Boy we took on road trips—our most prized possessions over the break—were abruptly replaced by bulky calculators with so many buttons I couldn't figure out what they did.

On our first day back at school, we awoke to the smell of eggs and longanisa, cured sweet sausages similar to chorizo, hitting the frying pan. Mum yelled up at us from the bottom of the stairs: "Boys, get up—breakfast's ready!"

I didn't think about it at the time, but we never used an alarm clock, relying instead on the smell of Filipino food to awaken our senses. Eventually Mum, who had an astonishing amount of patience with her two rowdy boys, would drag us out of bed, often switching on *Teenage Mutant Ninja Turtles* on TV to get us moving.

Mum, who worked for more than 30 years as a nurse, loves caring for others. She has an innate ability to make even the most miserable person laugh. She's the most charismatic person I know and exudes so much wisdom that I swear she's the Asian Oprah. When she speaks, everybody stops to listen. At the other end of the spectrum, when she says, "Clean up your room," you do it without hesitating, even though you're now 34 years old and it's your own house. I can't remember

ADRIAN BRIONES is the author of the best-selling book *What the Heck Is Filipino Food?*, which won a Gourmand World Cookbook Award. He is the publisher of the popular food blog *Food Rehab* and has written for numerous publications, including *Broadsheet*, *SBS Food*, the *Age,* and the *Herald Sun*. He has also been a speaker at the Melbourne Writers Festival, Writers Victoria, and The Emerging Writers' Festival and on ABC 702 Radio.

Adrian combines his writing and corporate leadership careers with work in the community sector, including heading up a training program for the disadvantaged. Most recently he was a key speaker at Voices of Young Leaders at RMIT University, providing mentorship to Australia's youth.

Mum ever being angry, except for the time I put my filthy sneakers in the washing machine (for which I happily blamed my brother).

We lived in Glen Iris, a hilly suburb of Melbourne, the streets resembling the steep roads of San Francisco. Our daily walk to school felt like fitness boot camp, especially after a lazy summer spent lying on the couch, playing games and devouring endless bowls of ice cream with turon, caramelized saba banana fritters with jackfruit. I took some to school one day to share with my friends. They reacted as if I were serving them food from Mars. (Alistair and I pretty much made up the entire preteen Asian population at school. In fact, that went for our whole neighborhood.) It didn't bother me too much, but like most kids, I just wanted to fit in. I often wondered why our lunch boxes looked so different. Why did we have to eat rice, when all the other kids had ham and cheese sandwiches? That changed when I started nagging Mum for sandwiches, although she filled them with Filipino food, like adobo, longanisa (Filipino sausage), and tocino (Filipino cured ham). This was a good compromise. Soon my classmates wanted to trade their boring ham and cheese sandwiches for mine. It was, indeed, a culinary victory.

I made it through much of the first day unscathed, but I wasn't too enthusiastic about the last period—math, the one subject most kids found unbearable, including me. The teacher, Miss Murphy, lived and breathed mathematics. She was stern but fair. The pen she kept behind her left ear always fell out as she wrote on the blackboard. She understood that not every kid was a math genius, but as long as you tried your hardest, she'd go out of her way to guide you. Often found tutoring my classmates after school, Miss Murphy was one of those great teachers who thought of their career as a calling. But that didn't make algebra any less awful.

Three o'clock struck—30 more minutes until school finished. My stomach growled so loudly that my friend Ryan burst out laughing.

"Miss Murphy, can I be excused?" I rushed to the drinking fountain, hoping that water would suppress my tummy growls. It helped, a bit. I spent the rest of the class wondering what Mum was making for merienda, Tagalog for snacks, hoping it would be ginataang bilo-bilo, a sweet Filipino snack of glutinous rice balls, sago (similar to tapioca pearls), jackfruit, saba bananas, and sweet potatoes, all cooked in coconut milk.

At 3:20, I started crossing out phrases in my textbook: "There are 20 passengers traveling in a train to London . . ." became "There are 20 bilo-bilo balls simmering in a pot of coconut milk waiting for me as I travel home. . . ."

At 3:30, the school bell rang—home time! A rush of adrenaline kicked in, and I ran along the steep streets, sweating profusely. Panting for breath, I flung open the front door like a SWAT team raiding our house. I gave Mum a hug and asked what she was making. "Ginataang bilo-bilo, son." My jaw dropped. Was she psychic? But that was just Mum, I guess, always knowing what we kids liked. (And what we didn't like but needed—Brussels sprouts!) A mother's intuition.

Before I could even gobble down the first glorious mouthful, Mum asked, "Where's your kuya?!" meaning "big brother." I panicked as Mum chastised me: "You know you should never walk home without your kuya." Just then, in walked Alistair. Phew.

"Why did you run home so fast?" he asked.

"I was really hungry," I admitted. I made another attempt to eat a spoonful.

"Uh-uh, not until your brother has some, too," said Mum, preparing another bowl.

"But Maaaa . . . ," I whined. My brother pointed at me, laughing. ◆

GINATAANG BILO-BILO

STICKY RICE BALLS, SAGO, AND JACKFRUIT IN COCONUT MILK

Ginataan *refers to anything cooked in coconut milk, whether sweet or savory. This snack is full of playful textures. It's the ultimate winter comfort food and not overly sweet, which makes a great excuse to have seconds. Other similar recipes call for saba bananas and sweet potatoes, but I like to keep it simple so the jackfruit shines.*

PREPARATION TIME: 1 hour
YIELD: 7 servings

1 ¾ cups glutinous rice flour

10½ cups water, divided

2¼ cups coconut milk, divided

¾ cup small tapioca pearls

1 cup coconut cream

1 (20-ounce) can jackfruit in syrup, drained and half of the syrup reserved, then sliced

¾ cup granulated sugar

Pour the glutinous rice flour into a large bowl. While kneading continuously, gradually add ½ cup of the water and ¼ cup of the coconut milk, until the dough comes together and is smooth and firm.

Form the dough into small marble-size balls. You should have 40 to 50 balls. Place these on a dry, flat surface.

In a large saucepan, bring 8 cups of the water to a boil over medium heat. Add the tapioca pearls and cook, occasionally stirring gently so they don't stick together, until they are translucent or rise up, about 10 minutes. Don't overcook the tapioca pearls or they will disintegrate.

Drain the tapioca pearls in a strainer and run them under cold water to prevent them from clumping together. Transfer them to a bowl of cold water.

Using the same large saucepan, pour in the remaining 2 cups of water, remaining 2 cups of coconut milk, and the coconut cream. Bring to a boil over medium heat. Drop in the rice balls and reduce the heat to low. Simmer for 15 minutes, occasionally stirring gently to prevent the rice balls from sticking together.

Reserve one-quarter of the jackfruit and add the rest to the pan, along with the sugar. Drain the cooked tapioca pearls and add them to the pan. Stir and simmer for another 15 minutes, until the glutinous rice balls have softened.

If you want the ginataan to be sweeter, add some of the reserved jackfruit syrup to reach your desired sweetness.

Scoop the mixture into bowls, garnish with pieces of the reserved jackfruit, and serve hot.

CHAPTER 7

DESSERTS

FILIPINOS ARE SWEETS LOVERS. This romance with sugar is evident during a meal, between meals, and at the end of the meal. There are several types of Filipino desserts: warm or cold, native or foreign influenced, custards or cakes, cookies or candies, and fruit or vegetable based. Two of the desserts in this chapter are spin-offs of the French dacquoise. Philippine-grown ingredients, like the avocado, kamoteng kahoy or cassava, and ube or purple yam, individually take center stage in the other three desserts in this chapter.

FINDING SYLVANA

T HE DOOR CREAKED. The wooden stairs squeaked. Our canines barked out a cry of excitement. Mother has arrived! The house was suddenly filled with activity and elation. Father revved up his energy and stepped out of the bedroom. My elder sisters turned into maître d's getting the dining table prepped up for supper. And we boys shifted our attention as our rumbling tummies began to anticipate Mom's cooking.

Amid this cacophony, I wondered, *What surprises could she be bringing us today?*

Mom taught Spanish and the life of José Rizal, one of the greatest Filipino heroes. On the side, she maintained a mini concession in the school canteen selling her popular cakes of cheesy cassava, cotton-soft chiffon, or chocolate fudge. Every now and then, she brought home treats from her fellow teachers or from peddlers. That day was one of them.

I dropped my homework and ran to the stairs to catch a glimpse of Mom walking up. Being the youngest in the family, I had my vantage point—I was always in front of the queue.

A Tupperware in a plastic bag hung loosely from her hand, and the familiar grin on her face was a telltale sign that something very exciting was about to be revealed.

As our dogs jumped playfully on her, she maneuvered out of their way, keeping the Tupperware out of their reach as if it contained a pot of gold.

With measured movements, Mom placed the intriguing container on the dining table. I immediately secured my spot beside her, growing obviously impatient and curious.

Born in the Southern Philippines, NOUEL OMAMALIN was offered his first international cooking stint in 2005 at Dubai's Burj Al Arab, then the only seven-star hotel in the world. Between 2006 and 2008, he became an executive pastry chef by virtue of his accreditation from Lenôtre Paris and a certification from the New Zealand Qualifications Authority. Chef Nouel joined a Middle Eastern airline in 2013 as in-flight chef. His cookbook, *Nouel's Nifty Chic Baking*, was published in 2017.

"Okay, you need to eat just half of it," she said firmly. "The rest goes into the freezer." Without further ado, one by one, seven hands reached in.

Ice-cold, firm, and clad in thin aluminum foil. One of my brothers asked, "What is this, Ma?"

"Sylvanas," Mom declared. "Sylvanas from my friend who rarely makes them."

A bite through the layer of nutty, toasty, crunchy specks of sweet crumbs revealed fragile, airy chunks of meringue that held with pride powdered golden-brown cashews. In between this meringue layer was a melt-in-your-mouth buttercream.

Even with the plethora of foodie pleasures she brought home, this was the one little surprise we all considered to be a great luxury.

I recall gingerly peeling off the casing as if I were defending it from the outside world—and probably from my siblings' sight. Every bite was a moment of true joy. I prudently and selfishly cherished it, knowing it might be months again before Mom could bring some home.

There was something about Mom that heightened our appreciation of food. Whether it was attributed to her heritage or simply a matter of familial destiny, the surest thing I know is that we all grew up gravitating toward food and would mightily argue that Mom's recipes were second to none.

The restaurant she opened, called Our Place, cemented my conviction that she was truly the home chef. She stirred us siblings toward a whirlpool of culinary discoveries, experimentation, and awakening. Food brought the family closer.

For good reason, sylvana became that proverbial delicacy crafted only by skillful hands, made with ingredients that marked extravagance in our time, and prepared using serious implements.

Mom became obsessed with recreating sylvana at home but with special considerations. It was chiefly made of cashews, eggs, and butter, ingredients that were either very expensive or not readily available in our local supermarket. Hence, she relied on luck and her budget. The high humidity and year-round average temperature of 90°F made creating sylvana a daunting task—the butter would melt fast and the meringue could easily lose its crispness.

Not all her experiments brought her success. Nonetheless, we enjoyed them anyway, remembering the same satisfaction as our first encounter. Mom, however, had unfinished business.

Our food-loving family went about with life. Things slowly progressed here and there, our neighborhood got busier, taller buildings rose, and the streets we once considered our playground became a dangerous pavement as traffic grew exponentially.

Two of my brothers got brave enough to eventually get married. My sisters, on the other hand, started working. Meanwhile, now in my early 20s, I got buried deep in cookbooks. It wasn't surprising that I chose the path of a chef—or, more precisely, that of a chef pâtissier. Perhaps the sylvanas had something to do with this.

Looking for new culinary eureka moments, my gastronomic adventures found their way home again. My every homecoming was marked by special gatherings with friends and family to savor my recipes, which were new to everyone.

Mom grew more curious and excited with every new recipe I whipped up in the kitchen: French pastries, American pies, and German baked goods, to name a few. She looked forward to my vacations. I studied and eventually lived in Manila, more than an hour's plane ride from Dipolog City, where my family lived. The newly opened Hyatt Hotel and Casino Manila was my first stint as a commis de cuisine.

One day, while busily preparing desserts in my hotel's pastry kitchen, the recipe for a French dacquoise came up. I watched my pastry chef weigh the ingredients, chop the hazelnuts, and sift together the hazelnut meal and confectioners' sugar to create the classic tant pour tant mixture. He whipped the egg whites and sugar until they became firm

I closed my eyes, relishing every morsel. The once-almost-lost memory of sylvanas resurfaced. It gave me goose bumps as visions from my youth sprang up before my eyes.

and glossy. He folded the ingredients carefully into the billowy mixture and spread the resulting meringue thinly on silicone mats. He then topped each layer with a generous amount of hazelnut pieces before they went into a huge oven.

The next day, I found the layers already in the form of beautiful baton-shaped gâteaux, lavishly smothered with praline buttercream. The pastry chef carefully cut them into bite-size portions. I heard a faint snapping sound as he applied more pressure with his knife. As I nibbled a piece, like a bolt of lightning charged with childhood memories, it conjured up the very same bliss that sylvana had brought into our family. The meringue layer effortlessly crackled in my mouth and the nutty, buttery taste of the icing enveloped my taste buds.

I closed my eyes, relishing every morsel. The once-almost-lost memory of sylvanas resurfaced. It gave me goose bumps as visions from my youth sprang up before my eyes. I saw how Mom's face had gleefully lit up as my siblings enjoyed their share to the full.

Aha! I thought. *Now I have a way to make Mom proud! I will make sylvanas à la dacquoise.*

I was ill at ease until my next holiday arrived. I began orchestrating the mise en place, applying the dacquoise technique, and replacing the traditional ingredients with the components of sylvanas. Mom couldn't help peeking through the oven's glass door as the meringue transformed into a crisp, light brown layer.

It was a triumph—especially for Mom, who may have finally put her own sylvana experiments to rest.

After a while, our family gatherings started to wane. I began to think I had better things to do with my time, and started focusing on perfecting my foreign recipes to prepare myself for an overseas posting. It also became more difficult to summon everyone whenever I returned home. My siblings had their own families to tend to.

As I traveled and gained more experience as a chef, returning home became infrequent and unpredictable. I became engrossed learning Parisian desserts at a Lenôtre accreditation program in Australia, studied artisan breads and chocolates at a French institute in New York, and furthered my plating skills in Tain-l'Hermitage, France. My heritage was unknowingly pushed back.

"Wing," my father said, using my nickname, one day when I was back home, "have you ever made Filipino specialties in your hotel?"

I didn't know what to say. I didn't consider Filipino sweets jejune, but it was difficult to find many people willing to try and appreciate our delicacies. Usually, I received an all-too-familiar jest along the lines of "You eat rice for breakfast, lunch, and dessert." My foreign coworkers had captured the Filipino's culinary penchant in one sentence. I could only laugh about it. I knew we had more to offer than puto (steamed rice cake), bibingka (broiled rice cake), or biko (sticky rice cake). But I didn't know how to place them side by side with popular Western recipes.

Taking fewer trips home and being the only Filipino in the workplace took a toll on me. On my days off, on several occasions, I shaped balls of baked meringue mixed with buttercream. Preparing sylvanas was sort of a therapy. It brought back childhood memories. It filled the gaps when I needed to be comforted and when homesickness struck. There were tough days at work, and I had grown too independent to rely on others for reassurance. I thought a call home might make my mom unnecessarily troubled.

When I shaped the sylvanas with my hands, it felt as if I were putting myself back into place. It was my healing process—allowing me to relive the comforts of home when I was too innocent to be bothered by the outside world.

Yes, those low moments of reflection and uneasiness somehow rechanneled my energies and helped me figure out how to best promote my heritage—now, Father had the answer he wanted.

Little by little, pichi-pichi, a steamed gelatinous cassava sweet; puto, Mom's popular cassava roll; and a host of other native treats crept onto my international dessert buffet spread, although not, of course, without my employing a twist or techniques to refine the process and elevate the quality. Indeed, my connection to sylvanas brought me full circle as the bunso, the youngest in the family, and a full-fledged pastry chef in international kitchens.

Sylvana needed to be where it should be—at the pedestal of international pastry greats! Technically, it shares the same soul as the Parisian macaron: a shell and a filling, made of ground nuts and whipped egg whites, requiring delicate treatment to produce a perfect piece. It is very much akin to my life's own musings: Mom shielded us with a sense of comfort and protection, filled us with warmth and relentless love, and allowed us to pursue our dreams while always being there to keep us on track.

Sylvana, out of reach then, is now a mission worth sharing, so everyone can experience what we felt when we first reached into that Tupperware and discovered joy. ◆

SYLVANA

BALLS OF ALMOND AND CANDIED LEMON PEEL MERINGUE
FILLED WITH COFFEE PRALINE BUTTERCREAM

PREPARATION TIME: 2 hours
YIELD: 30 balls

ALMOND DACQUOISE

7 medium egg whites, room temperature

1 teaspoon cream of tartar

5 tablespoons superfine sugar

¾ cup almond flour

¾ cup confectioners' sugar

7 ounces candied lemon peel, chopped into tiny pieces

BUTTERCREAM

1 cup minus 1 tablespoon granulated sugar

⅓ cup water

5 large egg whites, room temperature

¼ teaspoon cream of tartar

1 ⅔ cups unsalted butter, cubed and softened

1 teaspoon pure vanilla extract

FILLING

6½ tablespoons praline paste, peanut butter, or hazelnut spread

1 teaspoon instant coffee powder

1 teaspoon warm water

COATING

½ cup finely crushed saltine crackers

This recipe is adapted from the recipe in my cookbook, Nouel's Nifty Chic Baking. Sylvana is served frozen, so temperature control can be challenging, especially if you are in a tropical region where humidity compounds the heat. To address this, this recipe riffs on almond dacqouise in place of the meringue wafers that chiefly contain flour and ground cashews. This gluten-free version results in a nuttier flavor, and it is rolled into a ball, which almost any child can do. Of course, you can always use cashews. However, the additional candied lemon peel goes well with almond flour and mellows the richness of the treat.

Preheat the oven to 320°F. Line two baking sheets with parchment paper and set them aside.

Start the almond dacquoise: In the bowl of a stand mixer fitted with the whisk attachment or using a handheld electric mixer, beat the egg whites and cream of tartar on medium speed until soft peaks form. Gradually beat in the superfine sugar and continue beating until the whites are glossy and firm.

Recipe continues >

Combine the almond flour and confectioners' sugar in a food processor and blend until well mixed. Fold the almond flour mixture into the meringue. Divide the dacquoise mixture between the prepared baking sheets. Spread and smooth out the top. Distribute the candied lemon peel evenly on top of the dacquoise mixture.

Bake for about 30 minutes, or until golden brown. The center should remain soft. Remove the baking sheets from the oven and set aside.

Start the buttercream: In a heavy saucepan, bring the sugar and water to a boil over medium heat. Boil until a candy thermometer registers 245°F (soft-ball stage).

Meanwhile, put the egg whites in the bowl of a stand mixer fitted with the whisk attachment. When the sugar syrup is almost ready, beat the egg whites and cream of tartar on high speed until they become very frothy (almost to soft peaks). Lower the speed to medium and, in a thin stream, pour in the sugar syrup. After adding the sugar syrup, increase the speed to high again and continue beating until the mixture is stiff and no longer warm to the touch.

With the machine running, add the butter, a few pieces at a time. Mix in the vanilla extract. Continue beating until the mixture is very smooth. Set the buttercream aside.

Line a baking sheet with parchment paper or a silicone mat and set it aside.

Start the filling: Heat the praline paste in a small saucepan over medium-low heat until a candy thermometer registers 104°F.

In a small bowl, dissolve the instant coffee powder in the warm water and stir until smooth. Add it to the heated praline paste. The mixture will seize and become dry and crumbly. Break it into pieces and fold it into the prepared buttercream.

With your hands, break the dacquoise into irregular small pieces (about 1 inch). Fold the dacquoise pieces and the buttercream together until well coated.

Using a ¾-ounce ice cream scoop, scoop the mixture onto the prepared baking sheet. Transfer it to the freezer and let it harden for 15 minutes.

Working in batches, roll each frozen piece in the powdered saltine crackers and gently form into a ball with your hands. Place on the baking sheet again and freeze overnight. Serve cold.

THE PEAR-SHAPED AVOCADO

RODELIO AGLIBOT, known the world over as "The Food Buddha" for his dedication to his heritage and menu development, also had a television show *Food Buddha*, which premiered on TLC in 2010. He has been a frequent guest on NBC's *Today Show* and *Good Morning America*, as well as *The Ellen DeGeneres Show* and many more. He has been featured in *Food & Wine*, *Bon Appétit*, the *Chicago Sun-Times*, *Chicago Tribune*, and *CS Magazine*, which named his restaurant Sunda the "Best New Restaurant" in 2009. Rodelio has been a repeat guest chef at the prestigious James Beard House. He was born in Subic Bay, Zambales, to Filipino parents. The family immigrated to Hawaii when Rodelio was a child.

IT'S ONE OF every chef's dreams to open his own restaurant—to be his own boss and, most importantly, to cook his own food without filter and boundaries. Over 12 years ago, that dream became a reality for me.

Way before the ubiquity of social media, the popularity of reality cooking competition shows, and Andrew Zimmern's prophecy of Filipino food as "the next big thing," many Filipino chefs on both coasts of the United States were already promoting their culture through food. Most of these chefs had been overshadowed by a new wave of young hipster Pinoy chefs on Twitter, Facebook, Instagram, and food blogs.

My first menu that introduced Filipino food to the mainstream was in 1996, in San Francisco. I was a sous chef at E&O Trading Company, a pan-Asian restaurant where we tickled palates with wood-fired adobo pork chops and Filipino egg rolls. We pushed the flavor spectrum even further by using bold ingredients, such as shrimp pastes and fish sauce. When I moved back to LA as the chef of another pan-Asian place called Zazen, I infused more Filipino dishes and flavors into the restaurant's menu.

But it wasn't until I opened my own restaurant, Yi Cuisine, and wrote a menu that mirrored my biography as a young chef, that I completely embraced and promoted my heritage.

True, the menu at Yi's wasn't exclusively Filipino. Its cross-cultural orientation paved the way for other dishes, such as pan-seared sea bass rubbed with tandoori spices and raw oysters with mini scoops of wasabi sorbet. But it also highlighted my Filipino background with dishes of chicken adobo; oxtail kare-kare; my own take on sinigang, a seafood stew soured with tamarind; and many more. Instead of the usual crispy pata served at Filipino eateries, I created an haute version of the dish using Kurobuta pork complemented with a vinegar dip enriched with foie gras. For the finale, when the lust for something sweet became intense, my avocado mousse, probably the most meaningful of all my creations, reigned supreme as my signature dish.

I had never known avocado as anything but a fruit until we moved to California, where it is commonly used like a vegetable, especially in guacamole. Growing up in Hawaii, my parents introduced me to the avocado as a fruit; like all fruits, it was served in our home as a sweet. I was maybe seven or eight in Hawaii when I began to recognize the pear-shaped fruit for the first time—in the hand-carved wooden fruit bowl set in the middle of our kitchen table, distinctly different from a mango, guava, or pineapple.

I had never known avocado as anything but a fruit until we moved to California, where it is commonly used like a vegetable, especially in guacamole. Growing up in Hawaii, my parents introduced me to the avocado as a fruit; like all fruits, it was served in our home as a sweet.

At our kitchen table covered with a vinyl tablecloth (the kind that rigor mortised on the edges), Mom and Dad lined up short glass tumblers stuffed with hand-shaved ice. Dad picked an avocado from the bowl and sliced it in half, revealing its greenish-yellow flesh. He spooned the flesh generously into the tumblers, over which Mom poured equal amounts of evaporated milk and condensed milk. Using a parfait spoon, Mom mixed the concoction, creating tantalizing swirls in the avocado and milk smoothie. This had been my inspiration for my signature avocado mousse many years later at Yi Cuisine. The dessert is a piece of my childhood. It is from the love of my parents. It is me.

I had never written a business plan, let alone raised the $1.3 million capital I needed for Yi. I worked behind the stoves, headed teams of cooks, and reinvented menus of Asian dishes. But I was no entrepreneur. Both luckily and unluckily so, I embarked on my restaurant dream in the city where dreams come true—Los Angeles. Where else in the world would you meet enough people with the money to invest? On the flip side, most of the people I met in LA were impressionable and untrustworthy. The biggest challenge was to trust my personal judgment. Not to get caught up in the bullshit. Not to sell out my dream. And most importantly, not to compromise.

A few years after its birth, things went pear shaped for Yi, probably the only upscale Filipino restaurant Los Angeles had ever had. Despite glowing reviews and recognition as one of *Food & Wine*'s "Best New Asian Restaurants," the restaurant had to close its doors. Was it a reflection of Filipino food's unsustainability in the market? Maybe it was then. But there's one thing I'm certain of to this day: of all the restaurants I've opened, Yi Cuisine is the one I'm proudest of. I am proud of it, not for the accolades it earned, but for what the menu stood for and the story it told. Filipino cuisine, after all, is like the pear-shaped avocado. The fact that it is lesser known as a fruit in culinary preparations doesn't make it any less of a fruit. ◆

AVOCADO MOUSSE WITH RASPBERRY SAUCE AND LYCHEE GRANITA

PREPARATION TIME: 1 hour

YIELD: 4 servings

LYCHEE GRANITA

1 (15-ounce) can lychees in heavy syrup

RASPBERRY SAUCE

1 cup raspberries

¼ cup granulated sugar

⅓ cup water

AVOCADO MOUSSE

⅓ cup granulated sugar

2 cups whipping cream

2 ripe avocados

2 tablespoons gelatin

½ cup warm water

GARNISH

Fresh mint leaves

Before cutting into an avocado, make sure it is ripe. Ripeness can be gauged by the color, stem, and firmness. A ripe avocado will have dark skin, a stem that comes off easily when flicked, and flesh that yields when you squeeze it gently with your fingers. Be sure to make the mousse just before serving because avocado flesh darkens quickly if left out to stand.

Make the lychee granita: Purée the lychees with their syrup in a food processor. Transfer the purée to an ice cream maker and process according to the manufacturer's instructions until the granita is slushy with small chunks of soft ice, 20 to 30 minutes. Spoon the granita into a container, cover, and freeze until ready to serve.

Make the raspberry sauce: Combine the raspberries, sugar, and water in a food processor and purée. Strain the purée through a fine-mesh strainer to remove the seeds.

Make the avocado mousse: Combine the sugar and cream in a bowl and stir until the sugar has dissolved. Whip the sweetened cream using a whisk or electric mixer until hard peaks form. Refrigerate.

Recipe continues >

AVOCADO MOUSSE WITH RASPBERRY SAUCE AND LYCHEE GRANITA

continued

Halve the avocados and remove the pits. Spoon out the avocado flesh with a large spoon, being sure to leave the half shells intact. Scrape the flesh out of each shell and wipe the insides clean with a paper towel. Freeze the shells until ready to serve.

Dissolve the gelatin in the warm water. Purée the avocado flesh in a food processor until smooth. With the machine running, slowly add the gelatin mixture until incorporated.

Fold the avocado purée into the whipped cream until fully mixed. Cover and freeze until the mousse sets, 10 to 15 minutes.

To serve, fill each frozen avocado shell with the mousse mixture to resemble half an avocado. Pour the raspberry sauce on one half of each plate. Place a scoop or two of the lychee granita on top of the sauce. Set the filled avocado shell on the other half of the plate. Garnish with mint leaves and serve immediately.

ANATOMY OF A FILIPINO PARTY

KRISTINA VILLAVICENCIO, KATRINA VILLAVICENCIO, ANICETO COMIA REÑA JR., AND PAOLO DUNGCA are the creators of Timpla, a Filipino American supper club in Washington, DC. Timpla began with a simple vision to introduce modern Filipino cuisine to the city and has grown to incorporate storytelling, design, and art—alongside food—to educate others about Filipino culture. Timpla creates monthly dinners encompassing narratives about Filipino cuisine and immigrant experiences.

I N EXACTLY ONE HOUR, 10 complete strangers will walk into our Washington, DC, row house and experience a unique dinner influenced by our Filipino American upbringing. We call our supper club Timpla, a Tagalog word that means to blend or mix. Everything is ready: menu cards tucked into folded black napkins display each guest's name; tiny vases of fresh flowers and succulents dot the table; votive candles set in glass mason jars create a luxurious, romantic mood; lights are dimmed; and the sound system plays songs from our curated playlist of '90s R&B, hip-hop, funk, and disco soul.

As guests begin to arrive, the four of us introduce ourselves, hand out specialty cocktails, and open bottles of wine. Once everyone is seated, one of us explains, "Tonight's menu is a five-course journey reflecting our experiences growing up as Filipino immigrants assimilating to American culture. It depicts the adversity we and our parents faced coming into the new land and the opportunities we appreciate as citizens of this country." With each course, we explain the dish, its significance to Filipino cuisine, and the stories that inspired us to create it.

First on the menu is kwek kwek, a Filipino street food consisting of hard-boiled egg deep-fried in batter. We gave the dish a creative spin by coating the egg with squid-ink batter, cooking the yolk runny, and serving it with guajillo aioli and a sweet green papaya slaw called atchara. The second course is kinilaw, the Philippines' most popular crudo dish. When creating this dish, we combined the concept of kinilaw with the flavors and ingredients of another dish: sinigang—a sour pork or seafood stew. We use tuna, shaved radish, okra, jicama, and a tamarind broth poured tableside. The third course is palabok, a well-known rice noodle dish often served with pork, shrimp, crushed chicharron (fried pork skin), and eggs. But tonight, we are not using noodles or meat. Our palabok is uniquely vegan, with enoki mushrooms as noodles and a broth of other mushroom varieties that provide intricate flavors in the sauce. The fourth course is kare-kare, a staple comfort dish with oxtail, eggplant, and bok choy in a thick peanut sauce. Instead of presenting it the traditional way, in which the sauce sometimes overpowers the meat and vegetables, we let the ingredients shine and use the sauce simply as an accent drizzled over braised oxtail and roasted vegetables. Our fifth and final course—the one we are most excited to share—is the cassava cake, enhanced with candied pecans and roasted apples.

Each dish made its way into our menu because of its connection to our childhood; however, the cassava cake is the most special. It is inspired by the recipe of my aunt Tita Zen. When we asked Tita Zen for her cherished cassava cake recipe, she handwrote it from memory on a piece of scrap paper and wished us good luck. Our cassava cake, an homage to native Filipino cuisine, embodies Tita Zen's comforting warmth and positive energy. We had grown up eating cassava cake at every party on every special occasion with our kapamilya, or extended family. Today, it's an important reminder of both family values and celebration. The dessert is our way of transporting a table of 10 strangers in Washington to our family parties from childhood.

Growing up, family parties occurred almost weekly. There was always a reason to celebrate: birthdays, weddings, baptisms, graduations, debuts (the Filipino version of a sweet 16), first communions, or just the simple pleasure of getting together. These festivities were the foundation for strengthening family ties between and among multiple generations.

On Saturday evenings, we and our families would enter a house full of cheerful welcomes. Everyone who arrived was like a celebrity mobbed by adoring fans. Those nearby would crowd around the new arrivals with warm greetings, after which a tour of saluting everyone on the premises followed: trips up and down the stairs and searches through every nook, living room, basement, and patio space until everyone had been kissed on the cheek, hugged, or high fived.

This expansive expedition wound up in the dining room, where the party's host handed a plate, spoon, and fork ready with the words, "Oh, kain na!" Come on, let's eat! The eating implements were gratefully accepted as if they were a diploma at a graduation ceremony before we proceeded to the dining table crammed with food. Chafing dishes were filled to the brim with authentic Filipino putahes, or dishes, such as menudo, afritada, dinuguan, sinigang, lumpiang shanghai, lechon kawali, palabok, pansit, leche flan, buko pandan, ube, and the indispensable cassava cake. On the corner of the table, a large rice cooker marked the starting point. Over the years, strategies were formulated on how to best approach the buffet for maximum consumption, which usually involved the favorites-first rule followed by second and third rounds back to the table. After we piled the food high on our plates, we found our table of kumares—our posse—and sat down with them to eat and chat the night away.

Everyone in the family had a coveted cove to sit, eat, and chat. And although we would eat nonstop all throughout the evening and into the night, there was always space reserved for a generous serving of the cassava cake.

For the rest of the party, a cacophony of activities took place in the house: kids played with video games, board games, and toys; young adults mixed drinks and downed shots; the older generation karaoked to Frank Sinatra, the Beatles, and the Carpenters; and a group of titas played two tables of mahjong—the sound of shuffling porcelain tiles served as the evening's constant background music. The party would conclude at about 3:00 a.m. as we left in a sleepy stupor, joyful and anxious for the next one.

These relished moments in childhood kindled our passion for food. They were the epicenter of our understanding and love of Filipino cuisine, culture, and family. Many years have passed since those days, and many changes have happened: we graduated college, became workaholics, got married, had kids, moved throughout the East and West Coasts, experienced heartbreaks, and lost loved ones. But this important bond of family and celebration has been the best panacea for coping with all the changes.

The dinners we hold, which we call supper clubs, are an ode to those crazy, lively, and loud family parties. Timpla is our way of embracing our upbringing and weaving together our Filipino and American cultures. At these dinners, we hope that our guests, who walk in as complete strangers, will feel like they've become our kapamilya. ◆

CASSAVA CAKE WITH CANDIED PECANS AND HONEY-ROASTED APPLE

PREPARATION TIME: 1 hour 15 minutes

YIELD: 10 servings

Cassava cake resembles a denser, chewier panna cotta. It is starchy, moist, and moderately sweet. Unlike many Filipino dishes, which are of Spanish or Chinese origins, cassava cake is native to the Philippines. Its two most important ingredients—cassava and coconut—are indigenous to the land. Cassava, also known as yuca, is a root vegetable that grows in tropical climates and is abundant in the Philippines.

To add texture and give the dessert an injection of American influence, we enhance the cake with warm candied pecans and sweet honey-roasted apples. Some baby mint leaves and lime zest give this rich dessert a touch of freshness. Just as Tita Zen gave us this recipe with love for our supper club, we give you this recipe hoping it helps create new memories with those you love.

CAKE

½ cup (1 stick) unsalted butter, room temperature

2 pounds frozen ground cassava, thawed

1 (14-ounce) can coconut milk, preferably Aroy-D

1 cup evaporated milk

3 large eggs

1 cup granulated sugar

TOPPING

1 (14-ounce) can condensed milk

½ cup coconut milk, preferably Aroy-D

1 large egg yolk

1 tablespoon all-purpose flour

CANDIED PECANS

2 tablespoons unsalted butter

2 cups pecans

¼ cup brown sugar

HONEY-ROASTED APPLES

2 tablespoons unsalted butter

4 medium apples, peeled, cored, and cut into wedges

½ cup honey

GARNISH

Fresh baby mint leaves

Lime zest

Preheat the oven to 350°F. Grease a 9 × 13-inch baking dish and set it aside. Line a baking sheet with wax paper and set it aside.

Recipe continues >

CASSAVA
CAKE WITH
CANDIED
PECANS
AND HONEY-
ROASTED
APPLE

continued

Make the cake: Using a handheld electric mixer or stand mixer, beat the butter until smooth. In a separate mixing bowl, whisk together the cassava, coconut milk, evaporated milk, eggs, and sugar until well combined. Add the beaten butter and mix until well incorporated into the batter. Pour the mixture into the prepared dish and bake for 40 minutes, or until just set with the center still slightly soft. Remove from the oven and set aside.

While the cake bakes, make the topping: In a medium saucepan, combine the condensed milk and coconut milk and cook over low heat, stirring constantly, until the mixture thickens, about 10 minutes. Remove the pan from the heat and add the egg yolk and flour, stirring quickly so the egg doesn't scramble. Mix until creamy and fully incorporated.

Make the candied pecans: In a medium saucepan, melt the butter over medium-high heat. Add the pecans and toss until they are well coated with butter. Reduce the heat to low and add the brown sugar. Stir until the sugar is caramelized, then remove the pan from the heat. Spread the mixture on the prepared baking sheet and let cool completely.

Make the honey-roasted apples: In a skillet, melt the butter over medium-high heat. Add the apples and cook, stirring occasionally, until they are tender and soft but still slightly crisp, about 15 minutes. Do not overcook or they will turn mushy. Remove the pan from the heat and add the honey. Stir until the apples are coated and glazed.

To assemble, pour the topping over the cake, spreading until it is smooth and even. Heat the broiler and broil until the coconut cream is caramelized. Watch the cake very carefully while broiling—the topping burns very quickly. Remove the cake from the oven and let sit for 15 to 20 minutes.

To serve, slice the cake into 10 pieces and transfer them to plates. Top each piece of cake with some of the candied pecans and honey-roasted apples. Garnish with mint and lime zest. Serve warm.

UBE: A TASTE OF CHILDHOOD

MARK CORBYN was born in Hong Kong to a Filipino mother and a British father. He has lived there, in Singapore, and in the UK. Mark is proud of his Filipino and British heritage, and it was only in London where he really delved into his Filipino roots. Along with his brother, Mike, he cofounded The Adobros, a supper club aiming to spread the good news about Filipino food in a city where the cuisine is underrepresented.

LOVE ICE CREAM. I always have. Soft, hard, sticky, slippy, smooth, chewy, icy, melty; you name it, chances are that I will like it.

Growing up in cosmopolitan Hong Kong meant that I had access to a dazzling array of ice cream styles from around the world: from gelato to kulfi to dondurma to semifreddo to soft-serve and everything else. There was, however, one ice cream I truly loved, and still reminisce about to this day, and that was the ube (pronounced "ooo-beh") ice cream made by Dairy Farm. Ube! The humble purple yam from the Philippines turned into ice cream form! Disconcertingly purple, yet deliciously sweet and earthy, ube is unlike any other flavor I've encountered.

We always had a tub of ube ice cream in the fridge or, at the very least, a box of Neapolitan, that strange and most certainly not-from-Naples box of ice cream with three flavors lined up next to each other in distinct strips. Instead of the standard selection of strawberry, vanilla, and chocolate, the Hong Kong version had ube instead of strawberry and was all the better for it. The only problem with the Neapolitan box was that we'd eat all the ube ice cream first! As a result, whenever I accompanied my mother to the supermarket after school, I'd try to make sure that she bought the pure ube tub whenever possible.

Ube ice cream was a part of my childhood in Hong Kong. That all changed when, at the age of 13, I moved to boarding school in the UK.

It was one of the first meals in the school canteen, and we had all picked up ice cream for dessert—a couple of scoops of too-white vanilla ice cream, smothered in a sickly and rather artificial-looking strawberry sauce (throughout my time at school, this presentation never changed). To break the ice, we talked about what flavors we all particularly enjoyed. Some boys liked sweet and spicy honey and ginger clotted cream ice cream from Cornwall, others a sweet strawberry ice cream with chewy chunks of real fruit, one a tart and creamy rhubarb and custard ice cream from Cheshire, while the rest talked about the more prosaic vanilla and chocolate.

When it came to my turn, I proudly talked about ube ice cream. I was somewhat conscious that my peers in Britain might not be aware what ube was, but I was ready, and more than happy, to explain everything about the wonderful purple yam. What I wasn't quite ready for was the reaction: "Purple vegetable ice cream? Disguuusting!"

The look on their faces—contorted with disbelief and horror—was striking as they found themselves unable to wrap their minds around the concept of ube ice cream. No matter what I said, no matter what I explained, the very thought of putting a yam—let alone a purple one—into ice cream was just beyond reasoning. I even pointed out that rhubarb, too, is a vegetable, but they weren't buying it.

I was puzzled. Why would anyone think it strange to make ube, a vegetable commonly used for desserts, into ice cream? After all, in Hong Kong you had desserts with taro, black bean, red bean, lotus seeds, and even sweet corn. And even in the UK, you had carrot cake. But no, a purple yam was a bridge too far for the British. It looked as though ube would not be coming to the UK any time soon.

On my next holiday home, one of the first things I did was ask for ube ice cream.

We eventually moved as a family to the UK, settling down in the Surrey countryside, and with that I lost ready access to the sweet wonders of ube ice cream. I would have it only on infrequent trips to the Philippines

It wasn't just ube that I lost touch with. Every time I went back to Hong Kong, it felt a little less like home—things changed and became unfamiliar, friends moved away, and I felt a bit more out of place in the city where I was born and raised.

and Hong Kong, and it gradually faded away from me. Other ice creams loomed larger and more important in my life, even rhubarb and custard (to this day, I am a *big* fan of rhubarb).

But it wasn't just ube that I lost touch with. Every time I went back to Hong Kong, it felt a little less like home—things changed and became unfamiliar, friends moved away, and I felt a bit more out of place in the city where I was born and raised. To top it all off, those friends of mine who'd remained behind noticed that I'd even started sounding more English!

My focus turned more toward the UK and my life there—it's only natural, I guess, when you just want to fit in and belong. However, when I reflect upon my teenage years, it seems clear now that although I was connecting with my English heritage and my English friends, the identity I was developing looked and felt rather incomplete; I had forgotten about the Filipino in me.

My first girlfriend after university happened to be a family friend's daughter who'd moved over from Manila to study for her master's degree. Through her I ended up developing a circle of Filipino friends—the friends I now term my barkada—in London. This was a turning point for me, as it was the first time in years I was exposed to a relentless diet of Filipino culture (aside from having my mum's home cooking): the language, the jokes, the music, and even the drinks.

One summer, I went with my barkada to Barrio Fiesta, reputedly the largest annual Filipino festival in Europe. Back then, it was held in Lampton Park in Hounslow, an unassuming suburb on the western outskirts of London, and a real pain to get to.

Never had I seen so many Filipinos in one place in the UK; it was odd, this leafy park in West London playing host to tens of thousands of Filipinos, the cool breeze carrying on it a babbling cacophony of Filipino languages and the wafting scents of a dozen or so food stalls selling all the classics. It was a surreal, and surprisingly affirming, experience.

But when I saw the ice cream stall, my eyes lit up: right there, on its little canopy, it had the magic words "ube ice cream." I remember making a beeline straight for it, cutting through the crowds, and leaving my friends behind. Here I was, nearly 10 years since I'd moved to the UK, about to have ube ice cream!

My joy was short-lived, however, when I discovered that pretty much every other person there that weekend had already had the same thought. It was sold out! Crushed and disappointed, I tried to console myself by going for the flavor of macapuno, a special variety of coconut called coconut sport, and buying some ube halaya (jam) from the pop-up tindahan—but it just wasn't the same.

So what was a boy to do when his love of ube ice cream had been reawakened but he couldn't get it anywhere? Why, learn how to make it himself, using the jar of ube halaya that he had purchased—plus a healthy dose of renewed interest in his Filipino heritage.

Recent years have seen an importer bringing ube ice cream (from the USA, of all places) to Londoners in the know. Some restaurants now serve it, and very occasionally the Filipino stores in Earl's Court have a solitary tub in their pokey little freezers—if it hasn't already been snapped up by someone else.

But I no longer need to rely on them to take a trip down memory lane to the tastes of my childhood: with a trusty jar of ube halaya, heavy cream, eggs, a freezer, and a strong sense of the Filipino in me, I can bring myself back to those heady Hong Kong days and have a taste of my childhood in the tropics. ◆

UBE HALAYA SEMIFREDDO

PURPLE YAM ICE CREAM

Semifreddo is a type of Italian frozen dessert, often said to be like a frozen custard; indeed, one of the three main components is the Italian custard known as zabaglione. However, at the end of the day, it passes very well for a true ice cream. The greatest thing, though, about semifreddo is that it is extremely easy to make and, very importantly, does not require an ice cream maker. Having made ube ice cream without a maker (it is possible, and extremely good exercise for your arms), I can tell you that I am very grateful for having found and adapted a semifreddo recipe from FineCooking.com. While you can make your own ube halaya from scratch, it is simpler to just buy a jar.

PREPARATION TIME: 45 minutes + 6 hours to freeze
YIELD: 10–12 servings

WHIPPED CREAM

1½ cups cold heavy cream (see Note on page 222)

ZABAGLIONE

5 large egg yolks

⅓ cup granulated sugar

ITALIAN MERINGUE

4 large egg whites

¾ cup plus 1 tablespoon granulated sugar, divided

¼ cup water

1 teaspoon freshly squeezed lemon juice

UBE CREAM

1 (12-ounce) jar ube halaya (purple yam jam)

¼ cup heavy cream

Make the whipped cream: Using a stand mixer fitted with a whisk attachment or a handheld electric mixer, whip the cream on medium-high speed until firm peaks form, about 5 minutes. Transfer the whipped cream to the refrigerator and keep it chilled while you make the rest of the components.

Make the zabaglione: Pour 1 inch of water into a saucepan and heat it over medium heat until it steams. Reduce the heat to low and keep the water at a gentle simmer. Do not boil.

Put the egg yolks and sugar in a heatproof mixing bowl and place it on top of the saucepan, ensuring that the bottom does not touch the water. The point of this is to gently warm and cook the egg yolks without overcooking and curdling them. Using a wire whisk, beat the yolks and sugar, making sure to scrape the sides at the same time to ensure that the components are mixed and that a crust does not form. Do this until the mixture is thick and pale, like a batter. Remove the bowl from the heat and set aside to cool.

Recipe continues >

UBE HALAYA SEMIFREDDO

continued

Make the Italian meringue: Put the egg whites in a stand mixer fitted with a whisk attachment.

Put ¾ cup of the sugar in a medium saucepan and carefully add the water and lemon juice. Let the sugar become completely soaked. Heat the sugar water over medium heat until a candy thermometer reads 230°F.

Continue heating the sugar syrup, and begin whisking the egg whites on high speed, adding the remaining 1 tablespoon of sugar as you do so. Continue whisking the egg whites until the candy thermometer in the sugar syrup registers 251°F. Immediately take it off the heat and pour the syrup into the egg whites while the mixer is running. Whisk the egg whites and sugar syrup for 10 to 15 minutes on medium-high speed, until it cools and forms smooth, glossy, soft peaks.

Reserve one-quarter of the Italian meringue for use in the semifreddo. You can keep the rest in the freezer until you'd like to make more semifreddo or another dessert.

Make the ube cream: In a blender or food processor, blend the ube halaya and cream until smooth.

To assemble, line a 1-pound loaf pan with plastic wrap and set it aside.

Remove the whipped cream from the refrigerator. Gently fold together the whipped cream, zabaglione, and Italian meringue, taking care not to beat the air out. At this point, you can either fully mix in the ube cream or use it to create swirling patterns. Pour the cream mixture into the prepared loaf pan a bit at a time, alternating with the ube cream and swirling it as you see fit.

Cover the loaf pan with plastic wrap and freeze for at least 6 hours.

To serve, use the plastic wrap to help you lift the semifreddo out of the pan. Slice crosswise like a loaf and serve.

NOTE: Cold cream whips better, so keep the cream in the refrigerator until you're ready to whip. Chilling your bowl and whisk also helps.

A PERFECT ENDING TO A MEAL

"**R**ONI! RONI! HURRY!" Letty, our maid, shouted in Tagalog from the kitchen. I heard the quick slapping of flip-flops followed by the slamming of the front screen door.

I was 11 and it was the summer of '78. School was over and, as on all my summer breaks, I was homebound. The temperature outside hit a sweltering 105°F, and I was cooling myself in my parents' bedroom with the air conditioner on full blast.

I jumped to my feet and darted out of the room, startled by the commotion.

"What's happening?" I called out.

"Hurry! It's here! It's here!" said Letty.

Letty hailed from Leyte in the Visayas region of the Philippines, about a 36-hour voyage across the sea from Manila. She started with us as my yaya, or nanny, when I was seven and had stayed on since.

Twenty-something-year-old Yaya Letty, in a T-shirt and shorts, was as lanky as a teen, while her hair—salt-and-pepper up in a bun—was as gray as an elder's. She flashed her familiar smile, the kind that extends to her eyes and lights up her entire face.

Outside, a large cargo van was parked with its back door wide open. A deliveryman wheeled a bulky white box out of the vehicle. My heart skipped a beat. It was here! The appliance I had long been waiting for.

Yaya Letty led the deliveryman inside the house, then to the kitchen. A place had already been cleared for it. I followed the two of them, bouncing from foot to foot.

RONI BANDONG is a sales and marketing professional with a passion for cooking. Her personal mission is to make Filipino food known in the United Kingdom, where she lives with her partner, Steve McSorley. She is cofounder of maynila—an event company that specializes in supper clubs, pop-up restaurants, and food festivals serving modern Filipino food with a British twist. Roni's Filipino dish won the Best Alternative Christmas Dish 2016 on *Kirstie's Handmade Christmas*, which aired on prime-time TV in the United Kingdom.

The oven was my dad's belated birthday gift for me. He promised me he'd get me one when I turned 11. Four months late, but it did finally arrive!

As the plastic packaging was taken off, revealing a La Germania six-burner gas stove, oven, and rotisserie, I got ahead of myself and imagined all the yumminess I could be cranking out of that beauty: fancy Black Forest gâteaux; light, fluffy, to-die-for sponge cakes; flaky-crusted pies; decadent chocolate fudge–filled masterpieces; syrupy sweet and fruity upside-down cakes; chewy or crunchy cookies; cupcakes galore. *Sweet!* I thought. *It's going to be one heck of a summer! This oven is just the remedy I need!*

Being an only child, or hija única, had many plusses. Grand birthday gifts, as you can see, was one of them. I would also like to believe that being an hija única had spared me from the agony of sibling rivalries, the pressure of competing for my parents' attention, and the frustration of incursion on my personal space. Sure, there were minuses as well. For one, I was not allowed to play outside because I was alone; that meant spending my summers sheltered inside the security of our home, at least until my cousins bailed me out when they stayed with us for a couple of weeks. So yes, I may have occasionally thought the grass was a tad greener at the other side of the fence, where children ran, bantered, laughed, and played games like patintero (base invasion) or tumbang preso (knock down the prisoner) on the street. But I learned to fend for myself, found creative outlets to compensate for the absence of siblings in my life, and eventually mastered the art of keeping myself company.

Besides, I had Yaya Letty, my one true ally. She comforted me as an empathetic sister would when I was punished by my parents. Without a word, she'd serve me a slice of cake and a glass of Coke to console me, so I never felt that it was just me against the rest of the world.

The next afternoon couldn't come soon enough. The time when I, together with Yaya Letty, would put my baking abilities and my brand-new oven to the test. Chiffon cakes were a big thing, so I decided to go for an orange chiffon. Armed with Sylvia Reynoso's recipe, I embarked on my baking journey.

We had a small kitchen with limited countertops, so the dining table became my work surface. I sifted the flour and dry ingredients using a sifter my mum had bought for me. She said that sifting and refining the flour aerated it, making a finer, smoother mixture. Without really understanding the process, I followed my mum's advice and Sylvia's recipe to a tee. And boy, wasn't I glad I did. I would later find out that my mum was spot-on. Sifting was a prerequisite to a fluffy and light chiffon, as was precision in measuring ingredients, which I carried out with laser-sharp focus. Eyebrows knitted in concentration, I was a picture of a mad scientist working on a discovery that could revolutionize the way we ate.

Next to me, Yaya Letty, my loyal assistant, organized the wet ingredients, starting with the daunting task of separating the egg whites from their yolks.

After all the sifting, whisking, and folding, I poured the batter into my square tube cake pan. Letty skipped and hopped to the kitchen to open the preheated oven door for me. I walked gingerly behind her, carrying the cake pan with both hands. Careful not to spill the batter, I slowly placed it on the middle rack.

As magic happened inside the oven, Yaya Letty and I revisited our work area. The dining room looked as though it had taken a hit from a volcanic eruption! Volcanic-ash flour rained on the tabletop and the floor. Raw egg drippings cloaked the area near the mixing bowl. Dirty dishes and utensils smothered what had been the dining table. Ready to tackle the mess, I took one step forward and heard an eggshell crunch under my slipper. Yaya Letty signaled me to stop, as if I were about to tread on a minefield. "Leave this to me," she said, gesturing for me to evacuate the disaster zone.

If joy had a scent, it would have smelled like this—the lovely smell of baked goodness, a promise of something sweet and scrumptious to conclude your meal with a perfect ending.

While major cleanup operations were under way in the dining room, a heady aroma wafted from the kitchen. If joy had a scent, it would have smelled like this—the lovely smell of baked goodness, a promise of something sweet and scrumptious to conclude your meal with a perfect ending.

The scent beckoned my mum into the kitchen. She closed her eyes and took in a slow, deep breath.

"Mmmm . . . smells really good!" she said as she opened her eyes.

"Do you like it, Mama?" I asked. I tugged at her kaftan to come and peer through the glass oven door to see if my cake had risen. Crouched by the oven, it was my turn to drop my eyelids with pleasure and take a deep inhale, wanting to breathe in all that deliciousness.

Honk! Honk!

I bolted up and dashed out the front door. "Papa! Papa is home!" I squealed.

I pulled Papa by his arm to the kitchen. "That smells good! What did you bake today, darling?" he asked.

"I made you an orange chiffon cake, Papa!"

"Ah! We can have that after dinner!" he said, smiling.

In the dining room, restored to its predisaster state by Yaya Letty, our dinner was capped with an orange chiffon cake. Each of us, including Yaya Letty, had a slice. Before digging in, she stood at the corner looking content, smiling with pride, and watching us devour our dessert. When she ate her piece, she nodded her head in approval with each mouthful, echoing everyone's "Ang sarap!" ("How delicious!") before doing the clearing and washing up after the meal.

That was the first cake I ever made.

As I went on to high school, I expanded my baked goods to include drop cookies like snickerdoodles and chocolate crinkles, square cookies like lemon squares and food for the gods, cheesecakes, and many others, courtesy of my Betty Crocker cookbook.

One Christmas when I was 16, my mum asked me if I could bake blueberry cheesecakes and apple pies. I readily said yes. Little did I know that she was thinking of giving them as gifts. She didn't just want one of each, but 30 of each. So, there I was, mass-producing cheesecakes and apple pies. Thank God, I had Yaya Letty by my side, slicing up apples, giving me a hand, and cleaning up after me.

I now live in London. Yaya Letty is no longer with us. She passed away in 2015, without a family of her own besides us. She served our family until the end.

I am assembling a sans rival, a Filipino dessert layered with meringue, buttercream, and cashew nuts. Eyebrows knit, as I customarily do when deep in concentration, I slather buttercream on a sheet of meringue, then sprinkle a handful of chopped cashews over it. Bent over the countertop, I repeat the process layer after layer until I have a tall stack of cake. I straighten my back. With an icing spatula in one hand, I take a step back and look at my handiwork. I nod in quiet approval, as Yaya Letty did when she tasted my creations.

A gust of cold wind breathes through the open kitchen door. The draft induces a shiver. I look up, startled. For a moment, I see Yaya Letty standing by the dining table, her left hand resting on one of the chairs' backs. She flashes her familiar smile. I smile back and close my eyes. When I open them, a tear falls from my eye.

Yaya Letty hadn't lived long enough to sample my version of sans rival. But if she did, I know she'd be nodding and smiling in approval, not only because of its taste, but also because I have learned to clean up after myself. It would have been a perfect ending to her meal. ◆

COFFEE SANS RIVAL

MERINGUE, COFFEE BUTTERCREAM,
AND CASHEW LAYER CAKE

*Sans rival is a Filipino
dessert made of layers
of meringue, butter-
cream, and cashews. It
comes from a French
phrase that means
"without rival" and has
its roots in dacquoise.
It is very rich, so it's
usually served in small
slices and best eaten
with a cup of good
coffee. Classic sans rival
is vanilla flavored. As a
coffee lover, I wanted to
combine these flavors to
give it a different spin.*

PREPARATION TIME: 1 ½ hours + overnight to chill
YIELD: 8 servings or a 4-layer (9 × 9-inch) cake

MERINGUE

15 large egg whites

1 ½ cups superfine sugar

1 cup cashews, finely chopped

1 teaspoon coffee extract

BUTTERCREAM

⅔ cup superfine sugar

⅓ cup water

3 large eggs

1 cup (2 sticks) unsalted butter, cubed

2 teaspoons coffee granules dissolved in 1 tablespoon boiling water

⅔ cup cashews, coarsely chopped

GARNISH

Roasted coffee beans (optional)

Preheat the oven to 350°F. Grease four to six baking sheets. Line with parchment paper. Grease again and then flour the paper. Set them aside.

Make the meringue: In the bowl of a stand mixer fitted with a whisk attachment or using a handheld electric mixer, beat the egg whites on high until fine bubbles appear. With the machine running, gradually add the sugar and beat until stiff peaks form. Gently fold in the cashews. Add the coffee extract.

Divide the egg white mixture among the prepared baking sheets; spread thinly using an offset spatula.

In batches, bake for 25 to 30 minutes, until the meringue is lightly brown.

Remove from the oven and transfer the parchment paper with the meringue to wire racks to cool completely.

Recipe continues >

Make the buttercream: In a small nonstick saucepan, heat the sugar and water over low heat until the sugar is completely dissolved and the liquid is threadlike in consistency.

In a large mixing bowl, beat the eggs until frothy and light yellow. Slowly add the sugar mixture to the beaten eggs. Stir in the butter cubes until fully incorporated. Add the coffee mixture and mix thoroughly.

To assemble, cut or shape the meringue sheets to your preference (circular shapes tend to have a lot of waste). Determine the number of layers you want (at least 4 layers is good, but you can always add more).

Create the first layer by laying down a meringue sheet. Spread some of the buttercream over it and sprinkle with some of the cashews. Repeat this process until the desired number of layers is achieved.

Cover the sides with the remaining buttercream and sprinkle with the remaining chopped cashews. You may also want to top each slice with a single roasted coffee bean. Refrigerate overnight and serve cold.

ACKNOWLEDGMENTS

This book wouldn't have been possible if it weren't for the spirit we Filipinos call bayanihan, stemming from the root word *bayan,* meaning *community.* This trait is typically portrayed by a group of locals carrying a house on their shoulders. It's a tradition practiced in the rural Philippines, where folks pull together to lend a relocating family a hand. This book is a perfect illustration of what I'd dub as a global bayanihan—with numerous forces, not just from one village or town, but from all over the world, pitching in. Instead of a house, we carry our heritage. No doubt. The spirit still burns strong wherever we are on the planet.

I can't thank the contributing authors enough. You poured your hearts, minds, and souls into your work, and no matter how hectic your schedules were, you found time to respond to my calls, emails, and messages. Each piece is an integral ingredient to this book.

I would also like to thank all those who submitted to this anthology. We couldn't publish all the pieces we received, but your show of support didn't go unnoticed.

A huge thank-you to our food stylist and photographer, Rowena Dumlao-Giardina. Against all odds, you rose to the challenge with flying colors.

My gargantuan gratitude to John Birdsall for his very apt and moving opening remarks, and to Dianne Jacob, Matilda Butler, Ina Yalof, Alexis Williams Carr, Claude Tayag, Janet Rausa Fuller, Cathal Armstrong, Chris Dwyer, and Naomi Duguid for reading our unpublished manuscript and writing such heartening words of praise.

Eternal thanks to my sister and agricultural attaché of the Philippines to the United States and the Americas, Dr. Joy C. Javelosa. You've been my springboard from the time this anthology was conceived. I wouldn't have had the guts to embark on this journey without you. And of course, former Philippine ambassador to the United States Jose Cuisia Jr., former Charge d'Affaires Patrick Chuasoto, current Ambassador Jose Manuel Romualdez, and the different teams at the embassy and other embassies and organizations around the world, whose help and endorsements have been invaluable.

Sincerest salamat po to Dianne Jacob for all your help and for introducing me to Martha Hopkins, our amazing book agent. Thanks, Martha, for making sure our project found a good home. To the team at Agate Publishing, I'm grateful for your expertise and care in turning our manuscript into a book to be proud of, especially to managing editor Jessica Easto, whose eye for detail and organization skills impressed me immensely.

Bottomless thanks to all of you who helped bring this project to life: my friend Doris Somme, who gave me a hand in testing the recipes and performing ad hoc tasks; my husband, Leonardo Lauri, for his support so I didn't have to worry about making a living while I pursued this passion project; and my son, Raffaele Lauri, whose visual effects skills came in very handy. Thanks to Katrina Villavicencio for volunteering to design flyers, to Lisa Suguitan Melnick for volunteering to distribute them at the Filipino American International Book Festival 2017, to Fred Pallesen for offering to help me revamp my website, to Vien Cortes and UPAAS headed by Ton Garcia for endorsing the book, and to Alecx Mossige for immediately coming to my aid when I needed a dinuguan photo pronto.

To the followers of *My Food Beginnings* blog, Facebook page, Instagram, and Twitter—your likes, reactions, shares, and comments mean a lot. They keep me going, especially at times when it feels like nobody cares.

Most of all, thank you, Lord. To You be the glory.

INDEX